sowieso

A German Course for Young People

Workbook 1

by
Hermann Funk
Michael Koenig
Gerd Neuner
Theo Scherling

English language edition by
Joseph Castine

Langenscheidt

Berlin · Munich · Vienna · Zurich · New York

By
Hermann Funk, Michael Koenig, Theo Scherling, Gerd Neuner, Joseph Castine

in cooperation with
Peter Strätz (vocabulary)

Editors: Lutz Rohrmann and Barbara Stenzel
Layout: Theo Scherling
Cover: Theo Scherling, using a photograph by Flecks/Bavaria, Gauting

Authors and publisher gratefully acknowledge the critical assistance by Susy Keller and Maruska Mariotta (Scuola Media, Ticino, Switzerland), Spiros Kukidis (Moraitis School, Athens, Greece), Joseph Castine (Northport Public Schools, Northport, New York, USA), and Birgit Bauer-Berr (Zentralstelle für das Auslandsschulwesen, California, USA).

We would also like to thank all of the colleagues who tested **sowieso 1** in the classroom.

sowieso
A German Course for Young People

Volume 1: Components

Textbook 1	ISBN 3-468-96813-2
Cassette 1A (use with Textbook 1)	ISBN 3-468-47653-1
Workbook 1	ISBN 3-468-96811-6
Cassette 1B (use with Workbook 1)	ISBN 3-468-47654-X
Transparencies 1	ISBN 3-468-47656-6
Teacher's Handbook	ISBN 3-468-47652-3
Glossary German–English	ISBN 3-468-47660-4
Glossary German–French	ISBN 3-468-47661-2
Glossary German–Italian	ISBN 3-468-47662-0
Glossary German–Spanish	ISBN 3-468-47663-9

Symbols used in **Workbook 1:**

 Listening text on cassette 1B.

Printed on chlorine-free paper.

Printed by Langenscheidt, Berlin
Printed in Germany · ISBN 3-468-**96811**-6

Contents

Learning How to Learn: A How-to Manual for Language Learners

Tips, Strategies, Techniques

Contents

1 You Can Learn How to Learn

You have already learned many things in your life. Perhaps you have learned how to ride a bike, how to play a musical instrument, or maybe you have already learned a second language. Some things you learned quickly, others more slowly.
Some things you never seem to have learned. Our tips on "Learning How to Learn" are designed to help you learn a new language effectively and quickly. As shown in the drawing, there are many ways to reach your goals.

Every person has a different learning style. In *sowieso* we want to give you help and tips so you can find your personal path to learn the German language.

2 Self-Test: What Kind of Learner Are You?

We asked students: "How do you usually study?"

Exercise 1: Which of the following also applies to you? Check them off.

> I write everything down on small index cards. They help me to study and are very practical.

> I learn best when I work in a group. When I study alone I am often unsure of what I should do.

> I read a lot. Not only for school, but also for my personal enjoyment.

> Whenever I need to memorize something I also write it down. I remember things best when I write them down.

> I often do not know how much I already know.

> Whenever my sister studies, she listens to music. I need absolute quiet.

> Whenever I do not understand something, I ask questions. I ask my parents, my teachers, and my friends. Then I repeat what I have learned.

> When I study, I say everything I need to learn softly to myself. This helps me to remember things.

Exercise 2:
Ask your classmates how they usually study. You can see from the many answers that there are many ways to study and different strategies that help people learn. We want to give you a few tips that can be useful for all different types of learners. We hope the following example will motivate you to read further.

Exercise 3:
Cover the picture on the right. Look at the one on the left for 5 to 10 seconds. Close your book and write down the things you saw. How many did you remember? Now look at the picture on the right for 5 to 10 seconds. Close your book and write down the things you remember. How many did you remember this time?

Learning Tip ▶ If you organize the material you have to learn, you can remember it better. This is especially true with vocabulary.

In this chapter on "Learning How to Learn" you will find the answers to the following questions:

▶ Can you really learn vocabulary by putting the book under your pillow at night?
▶ How long should you study before you take a break?
▶ Five hours of cramming on the day before the test or ½ hour of study time every day – which is more effective?

3 A Time to Study – A Time to Take a Break

It is important to think about when and for how long you study vocabulary and grammatical rules. Many people learn best in the morning, but others can remember things better when they study in the afternoon or in the evening. There are, however, a few tips that are valid for all kinds of learners. Experiments have proven that you remember things better when you learn them just before going to sleep, and then review in the morning shortly after getting up. This is because other things don't get in the way of the material you are learning. Putting the book under your pillow won't help you learn, but studying right before you go to sleep will. It also isn't very effective to begin your studying right after you have eaten dinner.

I don't understand what's wrong. I studied five hours every day for this test and I still got fifteen wrong.

Many experiments have been conducted to find the answer to another important question: How long can you study with peak concentration? The results: The most effective way to study is in short periods of concentrated study, interspersed with short pauses. Studying for hours without taking a break is not very effective.

What does this mean in practice? Here is an example.

Thursday

3:30 – 4:00	Study German vocabulary
	5 minute break
4:05 – 4:35	Read Biology assignment
	10 minute break
4:45 – 5:15	Review German vocabulary and memorize dialog
	5 minute break
5:20 – 5:50	Do math problems

Learning Tip ▶ 30 minutes study time – 5 minutes break

Learning Tip ▷ Do not study similar material during the same study period. (For example, don't study your French or Spanish vocabulary words right after you study your German vocabulary.)

What works for daily planning is also good for weekly planning.

Exercise 4:
Look at Claudia and Petra's weekly study plan. Both are getting ready for a test on Monday. Who is studying more effectively?

Claudia	
Mon.	——
Tues.	——
Wed.	——
Thu.	——
Fri.	——
Sat.	1/2 hour
Sun.	1 1/2 hours

Petra	
Mon.	——
Tues.	1/2 hour
Wed.	——
Thu.	1/2 hour
Fri.	——
Sat.	1/2 hour
Sun.	1/2 hour

In both cases Claudia and Petra spent the same amount of time studying, two hours. Claudia studied a lot all at one time and learned the material quickly. However, she will probably also forget the material quickly. Petra learned the material more slowly and reviewed it more often. That means she will also remember it longer.

Students often forget the material they have learned right after the test. The result: They make the same mistakes on the next test. You must review the test material again after you have taken the test. This is true because the brain holds information better when you review on a regular basis. Reviewing the material you have already learned does not have to take up a lot of time. For example, you can spend five minutes reviewing vocabulary or grammar. You can do this on the bus, waiting in the dentist's office, or wherever. For this kind of review, "portable information" is a great help. Homemade vocabulary cards can be a big help. See next page for tips on using them.

Learning Tip ▷ Review regularly. For example: Look at the grammar table you made last week. Do an exercise from an old unit again.

Not only is when you study important, but also where you study. Whenever it is possible, find a place to study where you feel comfortable and where you can work undisturbed.
All of these learning tips are valid not only for learning a foreign language but also for other subjects. They are especially important when you are preparing for tests.

Who usually determines how and what you learn?

▶ The textbook. It usually determines the topics, the texts you read, the vocabulary and the type of exercise you have to do.

▶ Your teacher. He or she determines what you do in class and the speed at which you should go.

▶ The exam or test. It determines what must be learned by a certain time.

And you? What do you control? The Learning Tips in *sowieso* will help you to control your work and allow you to study more independently.

What do you really have to do, when you learn a language? You have to learn new words, read new texts, listen, speak and write and all the while use the new grammar correctly. For each of these activities there are tips and ways *sowieso* can help you. We will start with vocabulary.

4 Learning Vocabulary and Remembering: The Battle against Forgetting

The vocabulary box

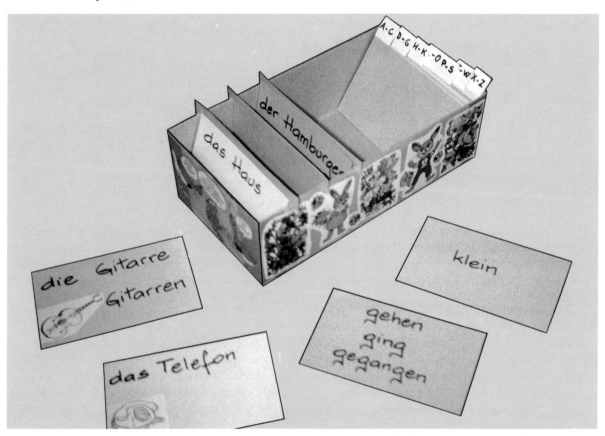

The best way to learn and to review vocabulary is with small index cards. You can use them anywhere and you can always rearrange them. You should build your own box for your vocabulary cards.

Write all the new words you must learn on the cards and place them in the first section of your vocabulary box. On the next page we will give you a few examples of how to write your words on cards.

Nouns

Front | Back

das Haus

die Häuser

the house

Verbs

gehen	go
ging	went
gegangen	gone

Adjectives

klein

small

As soon as you have finished making a group of cards you can begin using your vocabulary box.

All the cards go into the first section of your box. Now you begin to study them. The words you learn, you put into the second section. The words you still have trouble with, stay in the first section until you learn them all.

When all the cards are finally in the second section, you then review them all. The words you remember go into the third section. The words you forgot go back into the first section of your box. You continue in this way until all the cards end up in the third section. Now you have learned these vocabulary words.

⚠ Whenever you have many words to learn, remember to take breaks.

Making your own exercises with your cards

Look again at the examples on the previous page. Each card has an upper and lower part. If you cover the bottom half of the noun cards you create an exercise for the plural forms. You could also write the article (*das*) on the bottom half of the card.

For the German verbs you often need additional information: for example prepositions. Cards with such information on them might look like these:

Front   Back

sich interessieren für	to be interested in

You can then make another card like the one below and you create an exercise.

Ich interessiere mich ... Musik	für ———————— I am interested in music.

Here is an example for adjectives.

Das ist ein schön... Fahrrad	schönes ———————— That is a nice bicycle.

You will discover that by simply writing the cards out, you will learn a lot. You can make cards with your classmates and even exchange exercise cards. You can study together with your cards.

Learning Tip ⟩ Words that belong to a certain topic should be learned at the same time.

Exercise 5: Compare the two lists. Which one is easier to learn?

List 1

Thursday, airplane
Tuesday, Saturday, bicycle, bus,
Wednesday, railroad, Monday, Sunday,
car, Friday

List 2

Monday, Tuesday, Wednesday,
Thursday, Friday, Saturday, Sunday.
Airplane, car, bus, bicycle,
railroad

Many students believe that making vocabulary cards is too much work. Experiments have shown, however, that we remember vocabulary best when we study this way.

Exercise 6: Match the sentences with the percentages.

1	_____ of what we hear, read, and write we remember.	**a**	20%.
2	_____ of what we only see, we remember	**b**	35%
3	_____ of what we only hear, we remember.	**c**	50%
4	_____ of what we hear and read, we remember.	**d**	75%
5	_____ of what we read, hear, say, and write, we remember.	**e**	95%

Answers: 1d, 2b, 3a, 4c, 5e

If you actively use the new vocabulary, the chances of remembering it are even better.

5 Reading Faster and Understanding More

Now we want to show you how to read German texts faster and to understand more.

Reading in Geman functions the same as reading in English. In English sometimes we read quickly. We don't always read everything, but sometimes only that which interests us. We skim some texts. We simply do not always read in the same way. We have different strategies that we use depending on what we are reading and why we are reading.

You use the following three strategies when you read in English:

1. The Express Strategy — You quickly skim through a text to find out what it is about. You are not interested in details.

2. The Snoop Strategy — You read through a text, looking for specific information. The rest of the text is not important.

3. The Detective Strategy — You read the whole text very carefully, because all of the information is important to you.

You will find examples of these different reading strategies in the *sowieso* textbook and workbook.

Here are some examples of how your interests define your reading strategies:

▶ You are interested in soccer. On Monday you pick up the paper because you want to find out how your favorite team did. What do you do? First you find the sports pages and the scores and you look for the name of your team. The rest of the newspaper is of no interest to you right now. You use the Express Strategy and then the Snoop Strategy.

▶ You get a note from your friend. You want to know exactly what she wrote. You read the note three times. This time you use the Detective Strategy.

You also can see from these examples that the type of text you are reading is important. You do not read directions the same way you read a bus schedule or a love letter.
The text itself often helps your understanding. The soccer scores are in tables. If you know what a table looks like, you also know where you must look to find the information you want. The form a text has often tells you a lot about its contents. If you can understand some of the words from their context you may already be able to get the information you need to continue working. In *sowieso* you will become acquainted with many different German text types.
Very often you have a lot of information before you begin to read a text. For example, if you are reading a movie schedule you know before you begin to read that you will find the name of the film, the name of the theater, and the times the film will be shown. All of this helps you to read because understanding begins before you begin to read.

There are three phases to reading:

A Pre-reading phase

There are questions that can be answered before you even begin to read:
- Why am I reading this selection?
- What type of text is it?
- What do I already know about the subject before I begin to read?
- What do I want to do with this text?

There is information you already have, before you begin to read:
- Where did I find this text? In the sports section? In my chemistry book?
- What does the source of this text say about its contents?
- Is there a title?
- Are there pictures that go with the text?
- What do they tell me about the contents of the text?

B Reading

Pay attention to all the signals in the text!

Signals are important while you are reading:

The words that help you to understand a text when you quickly look through the text are important signals.

There are often some words in a text that will help you more than others. First you have to find the words that tell you a lot about the text. This means you should not read sentence by sentence but rather look for the important words. These key words will help you understand the text selection faster.

C Post reading activities

What do I want to do with the new information?
What is my next step?

There are many possibilities. For example:

- You could talk to other students about what you have read.
- You could write down some notes about what you have read so that you could use the information again later.

You will find more information on the subject of reading on pages 95–105 in this workbook.

6 Listening to Texts: Training for the Ears

Why is listening different?

It is more difficult to understand a foreign language when it is spoken than it is to understand a written text. Why is this so? When we read a printed text we always have the complete text in front of us. If there is something we don't understand we can go back to the beginning and reread it or any part of it more than once.

It is different when we have to listen. We hear something once. Either we understand it or we don't. There is also another difference: Listening is often "one way communication". It goes only in one direction. For example, when you are listening to the radio or to an announcement in a train station you cannot ask questions.

Therefore it is doubly important to prepare yourself for a listening text, since listening to the radio or even speaking on the telephone is a kind of blind listening.

A Pre-listening stage

You should always ask yourself the following questions before listening:
- Why am I listening?
- What is the topic? Top Ten List? Conversation?
- What do I already know about the subject?
- What will I be doing with the information I gain from listening?

There is certain information that you often have before you begin to listen:
If you are listening to the radio it only takes a few seconds before you know if you are listening to a baseball game or the Top Ten songs. You also often know what to expect, and can understand everything because you understand the context and can logically figure out what is being said.

B Listening

Pay attention to all of the signals!

Very often, when you are listening, the signals may be sounds and noises. These sounds give you information about the situation, the topic, and the speakers. They also create the atmosphere.

The content of many listening texts is easy to predict. For example: If you are listening to a weather report you know that it will be about sun, rain, clouds, and temperature. The text is therefore easier to understand. This same principle is also valid for other listening texts.

C Post Listening Activities

In everyday life …

What do you do with the information you get from listening?

- Perhaps you talk to others about what you have heard.
- Perhaps you make note of the information so you can use it later.

… and in German class:
In class you should actually do the same things you do in real life situations in English. There is however one major difference: Listening to a cassette is easier than listening to the radio. With a cassette you can go backwards and forwards and listen to certain sections as often as you wish. For this reason it is very useful for you to have your own *sowieso* tape and cassette player at home.

Exercise 7: Think about the information you already know about the following listening situations:

Top Ten Songs   *Announcements at the Airport*   *Telephone Information*

News   *Sports News*

How can you train for listening? Do you remember our three reading strategies?

1. The Express Strategy

You recognize the listening text, the topic, and the situation.

Example: You want to listen to the radio so you quickly listen to a few different stations until you find the music you like.

2. The Snoop Strategy

You search for specific information, and you concentrate on finding and listening to this information.

Example: You want to know the score of the last baseball game so you listen until you hear the name of the team and then you pay careful attention.

3. The Detective Strategy

You want to hear and understand everything and you need all the information.

Example: You are talking on the telephone to a new friend and she is telling you how to get to her house.

These strategies should help you when listening.
In a normal conversation it is much easier: You can see the person you are talking to and notice what kind of mood he is in or what kind of body language she is using. Most importantly you can ask questions whenever you don't understand something.

Basic Rule You can only learn how to listen by listening.

A few more tips:

Listen to German language radio as often as you can.
Try to use the listening strategies.
For example you should try to find out what kind of program you are listening to as soon as possible (news, sports, advertisement, etc.).
Can you get German TV programs? Try to listen to the program without looking at the TV screen, close your eyes or turn off the picture. Listen carefully and try to figure out what is happening only by what you hear.
Then try to answer the following questions: Who is speaking? How many people? Where is the scene taking place? What is the atmosphere like? What is actually going on?
Work with the cassette from *sowieso* at home. Listen to the dialogs and texts. Stop the tape at certain places. For example if you are listening to a dialog, stop after one person has spoken, and then try to guess what comes next. You should also try to write down important points while listening.

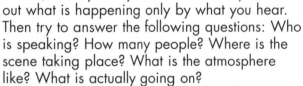

You will find more tips for "Learning How to Listen" on pages 106–111 in this workbook.

7 Speaking – Writing: Using the Language Actively

When we read and listen we "receive" language – when we speak or write we "produce" language. You will find more information about these activities in *sowieso 2*. In this book we want to mention the most important points.

Basic Rule ▷ You can only learn how to speak by speaking.

Many students are afraid of speaking German. They don't want to make any mistakes. This is totally wrong.

You should speak German as often as you can. Even when you are practicing your German at home, you should speak aloud. In this way you can get a feel for the melody of the new language. The two cassettes can help you.

A good pronunciation is just as important as using correct grammar or having a large vocabulary. Therefore, you will find help and exercises at the beginning of *sowieso* that you can use by yourself, even when you are not in class. The best way to learn to speak is to practice conversations with a partner – and you should not only practice in the classroom but also at other times. If you do not understand something – ask for help.

Writing helps you to learn

When you begin to learn a foreign language, you usually do not write much to communicate, but rather to practice the language. Do you remember what we said about the vocabulary cards? Writing helps us to learn words and phrases.

8 Grammar: Discovering Rules – Using Rules

Words are the building stones of language; grammar is the building plan. You need grammar to make meaningful sentences out of words.

However, the goal of your German course is not to learn the German grammar rules. You want to learn how to speak, understand, read, and write German. Grammar can help you to do this. Grammatical mistakes are not major catastrophes. The more German you speak, hear, read, and write, the fewer grammar mistakes you will make. However, if you speak and write little because you are afraid to make mistakes, then you will never be able to correct your mistakes.

Language books often contain many grammar tables. Students read the tables and learn the grammar rules. Later they are tested to see if they have learned the rules. We want to suggest that there is another way.

> **Learning Tip** ▶ Finding out the rules for yourself and making your own tables will help you to understand the rules better and make fewer mistakes.

For this we recommend the S-O-S Strategy.

Seek – Order – Structure

1 Seek
If you compare the words in different sentences, you can often discover the regularities yourself. For example you might notice that certain words always have the same endings, or that verbs always appear in the same place in a sentence.

2 Order
Similar words, word endings, and sentence structures can best be compared when you write them out in lists. In this way you can often recognize the rules yourself.

3 Structure
To better understand the regularities we discovered while putting things in order, it often helps to mark the structures we have noticed. Then you should try to formulate the rules in English. Only then should you compare your results with the rules given in your book.

> **Learning Tip** ▶ Write all your rules and tables in your notebook and always bring this notebook to class.

Making your own exercises

You can also make your own practice exercises quickly. Remember the vocabulary cards?
Take sentences from the textbook and write them with a grammar fill-in space. On the other
side of the card you can write the answers. Here are two examples of grammar exercises
on cards.

(anrufen)
Sandra hat mich am
Samstag …

angerufen.

1. Ich brauche ein …
   Computer.
2. Ich brauche ein… Heft.
3. Ich brauche ein…
   Kamera.

1. einen Computer.
2. ein Heft.
3. eine Kamera.

Amadeus,
was machst du?

Ich suche
Grammatikkarte
Nr. 718 …!

Learning

In order to learn independently you must understand how the book is organized, what you can do with the book, and how to find help. Therefore you need the following information about the way the book is setup.

Topics/Texts
Here you will find the topics and texts.

Communication
Here you will find what you can learn to do in the language.

Grammar
Here you will find the rules and examples: The building plan for German.

Learning Skills:
Here you will find the learning strategies.

There are two different types of units:

The regular units – In these units you learn new sentences, words, and rules. They appear so:

The plateau units – In these units there is no new grammar, but many review exercises. In *sowieso* 1 the review units are Unit 8, Units 15–16 and 23–24.

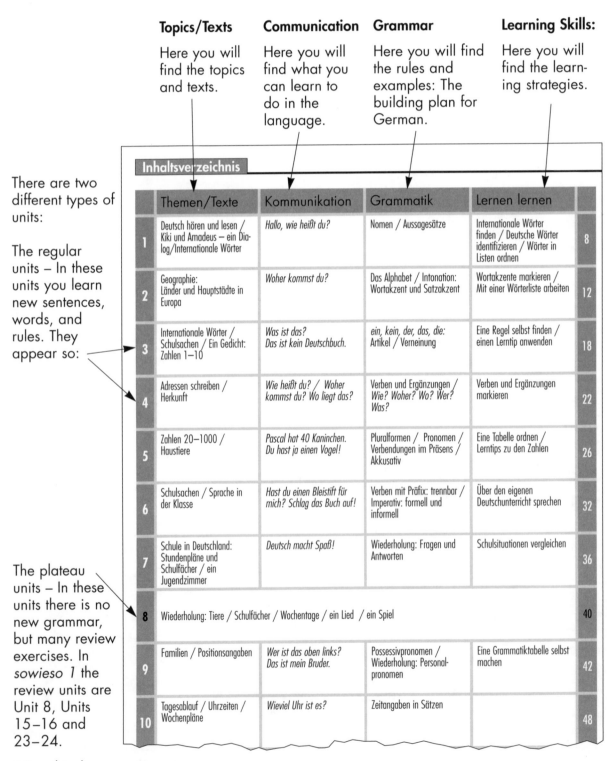

Inhaltsverzeichnis

	Themen/Texte	Kommunikation	Grammatik	Lernen lernen	
1	Deutsch hören und lesen / Kiki und Amadeus – ein Dialog/Internationale Wörter	*Hallo, wie heißt du?*	Nomen / Aussagesätze	Internationale Wörter finden / Deutsche Wörter identifizieren / Wörter in Listen ordnen	8
2	Geographie: Länder und Hauptstädte in Europa	*Woher kommst du?*	Das Alphabet / Intonation: Wortakzent und Satzakzent	Wortakzente markieren / Mit einer Wörterliste arbeiten	12
3	Internationale Wörter / Schulsachen / Ein Gedicht: Zahlen 1–10	*Was ist das? Das ist kein Deutschbuch.*	*ein, kein, der, das, die:* Artikel / Verneinung	Eine Regel selbst finden / einen Lerntip anwenden	18
4	Adressen schreiben / Herkunft	*Wie heißt du? / Woher kommst du? Wo liegt das?*	Verben und Ergänzungen *Wie? Woher? Wo? Wer? Was?*	Verben und Ergänzungen markieren	22
5	Zahlen 20–1000 / Haustiere	*Pascal hat 40 Kaninchen. Du hast ja einen Vogel!*	Pluralformen / Pronomen / Verbendungen im Präsens / Akkusativ	Eine Tabelle ordnen / Lerntips zu den Zahlen	26
6	Schulsachen / Sprache in der Klasse	*Hast du einen Bleistift für mich? Schlag das Buch auf!*	Verben mit Präfix: trennbar / Imperativ: formell und informell	Über den eigenen Deutschunterricht sprechen	32
7	Schule in Deutschland: Stundenpläne und Schulfächer / ein Jugendzimmer	*Deutsch macht Spaß!*	Wiederholung: Fragen und Antworten	Schulsituationen vergleichen	36
8	Wiederholung: Tiere / Schulfächer / Wochentage / ein Lied / ein Spiel				40
9	Familien / Positionsangaben	*Wer ist das oben links? Das ist mein Bruder.*	Possessivpronomen / Wiederholung: Personalpronomen	Eine Grammatiktabelle selbst machen	42
10	Tagesablauf / Uhrzeiten / Wochenpläne	*Wieviel Uhr ist es?*	Zeitangaben in Sätzen		48

How to use each unit:

In the upper corner you find the Unit number.

This symbol means that there is a tape of this section.

Here you will find examples of how you should write things down in your notebook.

Kiki and Amadeus will be with you throughout your study of German.

Important sentences and examples are always grouped together in boxes.

The vocabulary list at the back of the textbook will help you when you need to know the article, the plural form, or the pronunciation. You can find out how to use the index at the end of Unit 1. Look at it now.

aber (2); 7A2; 36
abwischen; 21A2; 96
achten auf; 19B5; 89
Adjektiv, das, -e; 17D18; 82

Exercise 8:

Take ten minutes and skim through the first five chapters. Write down the words you can already understand. We are sure that you will find at least one word in each chapter. Want to bet?

That is all for now on the topic of "Learning How to Learn". Have you paid attention to all the tips? We hope so. Come back to this section of the workbook whenever you need help. We are sure that these tips will help you to learn German.

We wish you lots of fun with *sowieso*.

The authors and publishers

2

B Thomas, Maria und Laura sprechen Deutsch

D

Ich heiße Thomas Helmert. Ich komme aus Deutschland. Ich wohne in Potsdam. Ich mag Hamburger.

A

Ich bin Maria Anderl und komme aus Wien. Das ist die Hauptstadt von Österreich. Ich mag Musik und Discos.

CH

Mein Name ist Laura Stucki. Ich komme aus der Schweiz und wohne in Köniz. Köniz liegt bei Bern.

3 Informationen ordnen.

Name	Land	Stadt	Interesse
Thomas Helmert			

Wie heißt du? Wo wohnst du? Woher kommst du?

Fragen und Antworten

Wie heißt du?	Ich heiße Monika. Monika.
Woher kommst du?	Ich komme aus Österreich. Aus Österreich.
Wo wohnst du?	Ich wohne in Wien. In Wien.
Und du?	Ich heiße … Ich komme … Ich wohne …

14 vierzehn

A

1   Many words in German are international. Can you put them together?

a *Information*
b _____
c _____
d _____
e _____
f _____
g _____

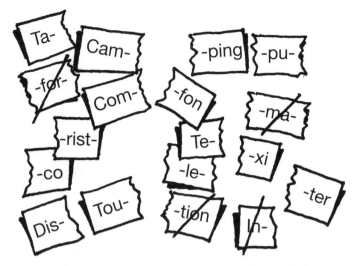

2   Write any German international words you know in column one. Write the English equivalents in the second column and any words in other languages you know in the third column.

Deutsch	Meine Sprache	Andere Sprachen
Tourist		*touriste*
Baby		*bébé*

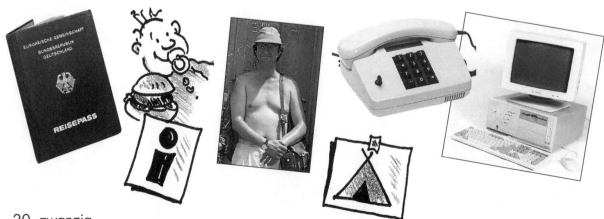

B

3 Was ist Musik Ⓐ, Sport Ⓑ, Politik Ⓒ?

◯ Conservatives in crisis

◯ EG-Konferenz in Brüssel eröffnet

◯ OLYMPIA 2000 IN SYDNEY

◯ Emma Eberlein: Neuer Star am Tennishimmel

◯ **Kanzler auf Staatsbesuch in Washington**

◯ Konzertprogramm: Mozart und Beethoven

◯ **München im Rock-n'-Roll-Fieber!**

◯ US-Basketball-Stars auf Tournee

◯ 5000 Teilnehmer an internationaler Parlamentarierkonferenz in New York

◯ POP-KONZERT IN DER ALTEN OPER

◯ **Auto-Rallye Paris – Dakar gestartet**

◯ Neuer Weltrekord im Marathon

◯ *LA CRISE DES PRISONS*

◯ UN-Truppen: Friedensmission abgebrochen

4 How much can you understand?

SCHWEIZER SCHOKOLADE
Die Statistik besagt: 9 Kilogramm Schokolade konsumiert jeder Schweizer im Jahr. Das sind 90 Tafeln oder 14 Meter Schokolade. Ein phantastischer Rekord!

Statistik / 9 / _____

_____

_____

_____

C

5 Sounds – Listen and then write the words next to the correct number.

① *Gitarre* _____ ⑤ _____

② _____ ⑥ _____

③ _____ ⑦ _____

④ _____ ⑧ _____

Gitarre · Auto · Telefon · Cola · Symphonie · Computer · Sport · Disco

6 Kiki und Amadeus: ein Gespräch. Complete the conversation using the utterances on the right.

Nein, Autos mag ich nicht.

Magst du Musik?

Ja, sehr!

Magst du mich?

Ich heiße Amadeus.

Ja, ich mag dich.

Ich mag dich auch.

Und magst du Autos?

7. Magst du auch Sport? Write the question you would ask your friend.

Amadeus mag Tennis.   *Magst du auch Tennis?*

Kiki mag Musik.   _____

Ich mag Hamburger.   _____

Ich mag Schokolade.   _____

Kiki mag Cola.   _____

Amadeus mag Camping.   _____

A

1 Countries and Capitals

			B					
			E					
			R					
			L					
			I					
			N					

◀ Die Hauptstadt der Schweiz
◀ Die Hauptstadt von Österreich
◀ Die Hauptstadt von Belgien
◀ Die Hauptstadt von England
◀ Die Hauptstadt von Frankreich
◀ Die Hauptstadt der Niederlande

2. Unscramble the country and city names.

NIESPAN __SPANIEN__   BINLER __BERLIN__

DANNLEG __E__   NERB __B__

EINLATI _____   RASCHUWA _____

NOLEP _____   GARP _____

SZWIECH _____   SPIRA _____

SCHANDLEUDT _____   SÜRBSLE _____

GEILNEB _____   HAKNEGPOEN _____

B

3 Correct the mistakes.

Ich heiße Deutschland. Ich komme aus Hamburger. Ich mag Thomas Helmert.

Ich heiße Musik. Ich komme aus Maria Anderl. Ich mag Wien.

Mein Name ist Schweiz. Ich komme aus Tennis. Ich mag Laura Stucki.

Ich heiße Thomas Helmert.
Ich komme aus Deutschland.
Ich _____

_____

_____

_____

_____

_____

4   Using the information given to you, write about each person and then write about yourself.

	Name	Land	Stadt	Interessen
a	Harald Meier	Deutschland	München	Musik, Tennis
b	Beate Schmidt	Österreich	Salzburg	Sport, Camping
c	Martin Müller	Schweiz	Basel	Hamburger, Cola
d	Heinz Elger	Deutschland	Hamburg	Computer
e	Silke Jensen	Deutschland	Bremen	Schokolade
f	Und du?			

Ich heiße Harald Meier. Ich komme aus Deutschland und wohne in München. Ich mag Musik und Tennis.

C

5   Listen to the letters – Write the words.

D-E-U-T-S-C-H   K-i-K-i

6   Listen to the letters – Unscramble and write the names of cities.

S-i-R-A-P : Paris

7.   A secret code.

NFJO OBNF JTU TVQFSNBO.   JDI NBH IBNCVSHFS VOE DPMB.

Hier ist der Code: A = Z   B = A   C = B   D = C   E ....

8   Make up your own secret code and write a message.

D

9   Listen to the cassette and write down the words. Mark the accented syllable.

Telefon / Computer /

A

1 Here are the nouns from Units One and Two. List them according to their definite article.

Technik · Politik · Hotel · Auto · Klasse · Schule · Computer · Disco · Kassette · Tourist · Taxi · Foto · Paß · Hamburger · Text · Sport · Ball · Automat · Tennisschuh · Bus · Information · Gitarre · Wort · Match · Judo · Lexikon · Maschine · Liste · Tafel · Radio · Baby · Buchstabe · Musik · Lehrerin · Schüler · Lehrer

der

das

die

der Paß, der Lehrer		

B

2 Was ist das?

 Computer oder Schreibmaschine?   *Das ist ein Computer.*

 Auto oder Bus?   _____

 Kassette oder Foto?   _____

 Kiki oder Amadeus?   _____

C

3 **Which words belong together? Use the list from Exercise 3A1.**

Sport	Musik	Schule	Sprache	Technik	Tourismus	Hobbys/ Interessen
der Ball	die Gitarre	die Klasse	der Text	der Computer	das Hotel	die Disco

4 **Which word doesn't fit?**

a Sport · Tennisschuh · Ball · Kassette · Match
b Tourist · Judo · Hotel · Paß · Information
c Füller · Bleistift · Hotel · Lineal · Radiergummi
d Buchstabe · Lehrer · Schüler · Paß · Schule
e Technik · Maschine · Lehrerin · Computer · Automat
f Gitarre · Kassette · Disco · Foto · Radio
g Sprache · Deutsch · Lexikon · Buchstabe · Tennis

Kassette paßt nicht! Σ

5 **It's not a dictionary, it's a passport!**

Ein Lexikon?   Kein Lexikon! – Ein Paß!

Ein Bus?   _____

Eine Schülerin?   _____

Ein Ball?   _____

Ein Computer?   _____

Ein Radio?   _____

Ein Wort?   _____

Ein Lehrer?   _____

Eine Schule?   _____

D

6 Zahlenrätsel.

10			Z				
20			A				
8			H				
12			L				
13			E				
1			N				

1+1			Z			
5+3			A			
4+6			H			
9+2			L			
1+2			E			
7+2			N			

7 Zahlen schreiben. Write out the numbers.

a *eins* – zwei – _____ – vier – _____ – _____ – sieben – acht – neun – _____ – elf – _____ – dreizehn – vierzehn – _____ – sechzehn – _____ – _____ – _____ – zwanzig

b zwei – vier – *sechs* _____ – zwanzig

c drei – sechs – _____ – achtzehn

d vier – acht – _____ – zwanzig

e 4 + 7 + 8 – 3 – 6 = _____

   20 – 15 + 9 – 12 = _____

   19 – 17 + 13 + 1 = _____

   14 + 5 – 8 + 2 = _____

   1 + 2 + 3 + 4 + 5 = _____

   20 – 3 – 6 – 9 = _____

   1 + 5 – 2 + 6 = _____

   16 + 4 – 15 + 8 = _____

8 Compare the way numbers are written in German, English, and any other languages you may know.

Deutsch	Englisch	Andere Sprachen
dreizehn		
vierzehn		
fünfzehn		
sechzehn		
siebzehn		
achtzehn		
neunzehn		

A

 1 Write two dialogs using the given utterances.

Woher kommst du?   Wie geht's?

Hallo Peter.   Aus Monopoli.   In Italien. Bei Bari.

Wo liegt denn das?   Auch gut, danke.

Gut, danke. Und Ihnen?   Guten Morgen, Herr Müller.

Eva:

_____?

Aldo:

_____.

_____?   _____.

Herr Müller:

_____.

Peter:

_____.

_____?

_____?

_____.

B

2 Reading and writing addresses.

Die Adresse in Deutschland

Fritz (1) Gruber (2)

Blumenstraße (3) 34 (4)
76835 (5) Hainfeld (6)

Die Adresse in meinem Land

(1): der Vorname   (4): die Hausnummer
(2): der Name   (5): die Postleitzahl
(3): die Straße   (6): der Ort

3 Write the addresses on the correct cards.

Kurt Müller
Schillerweg 15
67471 Elmstein
Tel.: 43 58 14

Lothar Kulle
Meisenweg 7
36142 Tann
Tel.: 34 56 78

Renate Schubert
Am Wall 7
23715 Bosau
Tel.: 97 68 74

Helga Wenk
Dorfstraße 2
76872 Minfeld
Tel.: 22 17 65

Meine Telefonnummer ist drei-vier-fünf-sechs-sieben-acht.

Name:
Straße:
Stadt:

Lothar Kulle

Meine Telefonnummer ist zwei-zwei-eins-sieben-sechs-fünf.

Name:
Straße:
Stadt:

Meine Nummer ist vier-drei- -fünf-acht-eins-vier.

Name:
Straße:
Stadt:

Meine Nummer ist neun-sieben-sechs-acht-sieben-vier.

Name:
Straße:
Stadt:

C

4 Circle all the verbs.

Ich (heiße) Aldo. Ich komme aus Monopoli. Das ist bei Bari. Ich wohne jetzt in Frankfurt.

Ich bin in Klasse 7a. Ich spreche gut Deutsch. Ich spiele Fußball. Ich mag Popmusik.

Sie heißt Carola. Sie kommt aus Ascona. Das ist in der Schweiz. Sie spricht Deutsch

und Italienisch. Sie lernt Englisch. Sie ist dreizehn.

D

5 Questions with interrogatives.

People: wer?

Kiki, Amadeus
Aldo, Carola

Things: was?

ein Buch, ein Ball
eine Tafel, ...

Wer ist das ___ ?

_____ ?

_____ ?

_____ ?

_____ ?

6 Questions without interrogatives. Write out the questions.

Sprichst du	Tennis
Lernst du	Deutsch
Magst du	in Deutschland
Wohnst du	Englisch

Sprichst du Deutsch?

_____

_____

_____

_____

A

1 Write down the names for these "compound" animals.

das Pferd
das Kamel

2 Put the parts together and write the correct words.

T	

Fa-
-fel
Ta-
-to
Lö-
-mi-
Ot-
-fant
neun
-lie
Ei
-we
Ele-

B

3   How many animal names can you find?

PAPAHUN**PIF**ININCHKATKANAVO**PFE**

4   Listen to the cassette and write down the key words.

	Name	Alter	Wohnort	Hobbys/Tiere
Text 1				
Text 2				
Text 3				

5   Write about yourself.

Wie heißt du?   _____

Wie alt bist du?   _____

Wo wohnst du (Land/Stadt)?   _____

Welche Hobbys hast du?   _____

Magst du Tiere?   _____

Hast du Tiere?   _____

C

6   Listen to the cassette and fill in the blanks.

Text 1   Ich bin Fredo. Ich bin der _____ von Daniel. Daniel _____ mein Freund. Ich bin _____ Cocker. Ich bin drei _____ alt. Ich _____ Schuhe, aber ich mag keine _____.

Text 2   Ich bi ____ der Af____ Charlie. I____ kom____ aus Afrika. Ich wohn____ in Hamburg, i____ Zoo. Ich hab____ zwei Hobbys: Ich sp____ Gita____ und ich e____ Ba_____.

Text 3   Ich bi____ der Comp_____ von Dan____. Ich sa____ zu Dan____: „Guten Mor____!" Er is____ nicht i____ der Schu____. Ich ma____ die Haus_____. Ich schre____ eine Wörter_____. Ich le____ den Tex____. Ich le____ ein Ged____.

7 Wie viele Tiere hat Amadeus?

zwei Fische

_____

_____

Was ist in der Klasse von Kiki?

drei Bilder

_____

_____

D/E

8 What does Daniel have?

Daniel hat einen Computer.

_____

_____

_____

What does he not have?

Daniel hat keine Brille.

_____

_____

_____

9 What do you have? What don't you have? Listen to the cassette and write the answers in your notebook.

Nein, ich habe keine Giraffe.

10 Listen to the cassette and fill in the blanks.

a $15 + 3 + \_\_\_ + 4 + \_\_\_ = 30$

b $2 + \_\_\_ + 6 + \_\_\_ - \_\_\_ + 3 = 10$

c $20 + \_\_\_ + \_\_\_ - 40 - 12 = 50$

d $22 + 44 - 63 + \_\_\_ - 31 = 0$

e $97 - 79 + 86 + 32 - \_\_\_ = 45$

f $151 + 326 + 242 - 428 = \_\_\_$

g $222 + 333 + 444 = \_\_\_$

h $999 - 106 + \_\_\_ - 653 = 500$

i $\_\_\_ + 202 + 303 + 204 = \_\_\_$

j $909 - \_\_\_ + 505 - 333 = \_\_\_$

A

1 German class – French class. Write (in German) what could happen in a French class.

Die Deutschstunde	Die Französischstunde
Der Lehrer kommt.	_____
Er sagt: „Guten Morgen!"	_____
Er spricht Deutsch.	_____
Er fragt – die Schüler antworten.	_____
Er hilft.	_____
Er korrigiert.	_____
Er liest vor.	_____
Er sagt: „Lernt die Wörter!"	_____
Er sagt: „Auf Wiedersehen!"	_____
Er geht.	_____

2 **Das sagt Amadeus:**

„Mathe _____ blöd. Ich _____ Englisch gut.

Französisch _____ ich nicht. Sport _____ super.

Noten _____ ich nicht. Schule _____ langweilig.

Tennis _____ ich toll. Fußball _____ ich nicht so gut."

3 **Was sagst du? Schreibe 5 Sätze.**

4 **Match the words in the two columns.**

vorlesen	Tennis
aufschlagen	Bücher
hören	Radio
geben	Diktate
spielen	Vokabeln
diktieren	Sätze
korrigieren	Texte
aufschreiben	Wörter
sprechen	Comics
lesen	Noten

Tennis spielen _____

_____

_____

_____

_____

5 **Wer sagt was? Listen to the cassette and check the correct column.**

		Schülerin/ Schüler	Lehrerin/ Lehrer
a	den Satz an die Tafel schreiben		
b	etwas lauter sprechen		
c	den Text von Seite 42 lesen		
d	das Wort an die Tafel schreiben		
e	die Kassette hören		
f	den Satz vorlesen		
g	langsam sprechen		
h	den Satz ergänzen		
i	das Buch aufschlagen		
j	das Wort wiederholen		

6 **Listen to the cassette again. This time write out the sentences in your notebook.**

7 **Was sagen die Tiere? Be creative.**

Wo sind die Bananen?

A

1 Schule: Wie heißen die Wörter?

B

2 Stefans Stundenplan. Listen to the cassette. Fill in the blanks and answer the questions.

Stefan hat 5 Tage _____. Am Samstag hat er keinen _____.

a Welche _____ hat er am Montag?   **b** Wann hat er _____?

c Hat er auch _____?   **d** Was hat er am _____?

e Wann hat er fünf _____?

Antworten

a _____

b _____

c _____

d _____

e _____

3 Create your ideal weekly schedule.

Montag	Dienstag	Mittwoch	Donnerstag	Freitag	Samstag

4 Listen to the cassette and fill in the blanks with the information you hear.

Am Montag mache ich _____. Am _____ spiele ich

_____. Am Mittwoch gehe ich mit meinem _____ spazieren.

Am Donnerstag spiele ich _____. Am Freitag machen wir zu Hause eine

_____. Am _____ mache ich nichts. Am Sonntag gehen wir in

den _____. Am liebsten mag ich die _____.

5 Was machst du am ...? Schreibe einen Text.

Montag?   Hausaufgaben machen
Dienstag?   Musik machen
Mittwoch?   Freundin/Freund kommt
Donnerstag?   Gitarre/Tennis spielen
Freitag?   Wörter lernen
Samstag?   Buch lesen
Sonntag?   spazieren gehen
                 nichts machen

_____

_____

_____

_____

_____

_____

Review exercises for Units 1–7

1   What can you say? How do you ask?

1   Write the answers.

a

Club der Deutschlernfans international
Clubausweis

Name: _____

Adresse: _____

_____

_____

Telefonnummer: _____

Klasse: _____

b Kiki sagt, sie mag Fußball.
Du sagst, du findest das
auch (++).

_____

c Ein Junge sagt: „Ich heiße Amadeus."
Du verstehst seinen Namen nicht.

_____

d Kiki fragt: „Woher kommst du?"

_____

„Sprichst du Deutsch?"

_____

e Amadeus fragt: „Bist du 20?"

_____

f Buchstabiere deinen Namen laut.
Schreibe die B-U-C-H-S-T-A-B-E-N
auf.

_____

g Du kennst ein Wort nicht.
Frag auf deutsch.

_____

h Kiki fragt dich: „Wie geht's?"   (+): _____

(–): _____

i Amadeus sagt: „Tennis ist klasse!"
Du findest das nicht.

_____

j Wie findest du diese Übung?

_____

2 Vocabulary

2 Sport, Musik und Schule: Welche Wörter kennst du? Create word fields for sport, music, and school.

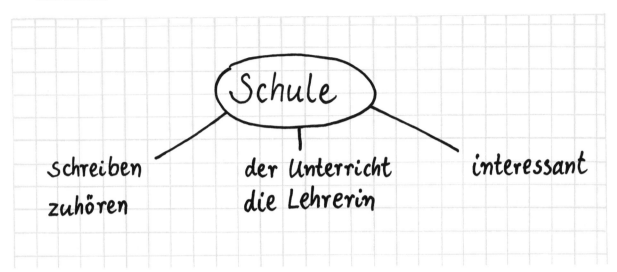

3 One word in each row does not fit.

a Lehrerin, Schüler, Lexikon, <u>Hotel,</u> Tafel

b Text, Tennis, Wort, Satz, Buch

c Fußball, Sport, Musik, Tennis, Banane

d Auto, Löwe, Katze, Hund, Pinguin

e vorlesen, nachschlagen, hören, vorspielen, aufpassen

f Amadeus, Antwort, auch, Artikel, Auto

4 Match the words in the two columns.

Text	hören
Kassette	schreiben
Radio	lesen
Diktat	sprechen
Wort	lernen
Lied	spielen
Tennis	buchstabieren
Dialog	singen

5 Complete the sentences using the word that fits from the list on the right.

a Woher _____ du?

kommst · heißt · wohnst · gehst

b Wer bist _____?

du · er · sie · ich

c Berlin _____ in Deutschland.

wohnst · kommt · liegt · heißt

d Die Katze _____ keine Hunde.

spricht · ißt · macht · mag

e Die _____ kommen in die Klasse.

Katzen · Bücher · Schüler · Taschen

f „Schlagt die Bücher _____!"

ab · auf · nach · an

g Das finde ich _____.

gut · super · blöd · prima

h Das ist _____.

langweilig · toll · blöd

i achtundvierzig, _____
fünfzig, einundfünfzig

sechsundvierzig · siebenundvierzig ·
neunundvierzig · zweiundfünfzig

j Montag, _____, Mittwoch

Dienstag · Donnerstag · Freitag · Samstag ·
Sonntag

3 Pronunciation/Intonation

6 Long or short? Put a check in the correct column.

	lang __	kurz ●
Stadt		
Staat		
Land		
Ton		
wohnen		
liegen		
ist		
kommen		
Disco		
gut		

7 Word intonation – mark the stressed syllable.

Musik Telefon Papagei Dialog Diktat Information Begrüßung Bettina
Gedicht Griechenland Deutschland international

4 Spelling

8 Complete and write the words that are missing letters.

Guten Morg①! Ich hei②e
Ulla Klein. Ich wo③ne in
Berli④. Das ist die
Hauptst⑤dt von
Deut⑥chland. Mein Hobb⑦
ist Te⑧is. Fu⑨ball finde ich
auch gu⑩!

① _____   ⑥ _____

② _____   ⑦ _____

③ _____   ⑧ _____

④ _____   ⑨ _____

⑤ _____   ⑩ _____

5 Grammar

9 Match the nouns with the correct article.

der   das   die

Paß
Satz
Buch
Text
Gitarre
Pause
Brille
Bleistift
Auto
Note
Heft

_____   _____   _____

_____   _____   _____

_____   _____   _____

_____   _____   _____

10 What is the plural form?

der Sportschuh	*die Sportschuhe*	die Tafel	_____
das Auto	_____	der Computer	_____
der Radiergummi	_____	der Lehrer	_____
die Turnhose	_____	die Katze	_____
das Lineal	_____	die Lehrerin	_____

11 What are the correct endings?

Ich habe ein____ Hund. Er heiß__ Fredo. Er mag Bananen. Er mag kein__ Katzen. Er is__

drei Jahre alt. Er hat zwei Freund__ Bonni und Clyde. Sie sin__ Bobtails. Sie komm____

aus England. Sie mögen kein____ Salat. Aber sie mögen Küh___.

12 True or false? Listen to the cassette and place a check in the correct column.

René hat Haustiere.

	richtig	falsch
Rico und Lora sind zwei Hunde.		
Rico sagt: „Tschüs, Tschüs".		
Lora ist 35 Jahre alt.		
Rico ist 68 Jahre alt.		
Rico mag Salat.		
Lora mag Hamburger und Salat.		

13 Read the text and then match the sentence parts.

Kiki und Amadeus im Deutschunterricht

Kiki und Amadeus sind in Klasse 7. Am Montag haben sie 2 Stunden Deutsch. Kiki mag Deutsch, Amadeus nicht. Amadeus macht immer Fehler!
Er sagt: „Ich mögen dich!" Kiki korrigiert ihn: „Das heißt: ‚Ich mag dich!' " –
„Ich dich auch!" sagt Amadeus – „Das sage ich doch!".
Kiki sagt zu Amadeus: „Schreib den Text auf!"
Und was macht Amadeus? Er holt ein Buch!
Kiki fragt Amadeus: „Wie alt bist du?", Amadeus antwortet: „Ja, gut!"
Kiki fragt: „Wo ist das Deutschbuch?", Amadeus antwortet: „Am Montag."
Kiki sagt zu Amadeus: „Du bist blöd!", Amadeus antwortet: „Ja, vielen Dank!"
„Du, Kiki", sagt Amadeus am Dienstag.
„Was ist?" fragt Kiki.
„Hier ist ein Gedicht", sagt Amadeus, „ein Dienstags-Gedicht." Es ist für Frau Bender, die Deutschlehrerin:
> Ich Amadeus heißen
> und viele deutsche Wörter weißen!
„Frau Bender findet das sicher ganz klasse!" sagt Kiki. „Du bekommst in Deutsch eine gute Note, eine Eins!"

Kiki und Amadeus sind	falsch.
Amadeus macht	gut Deutsch.
Amadeus versteht	nicht gut Deutsch.
Kiki versteht	in Klasse sieben.
Amadeus antwortet	viele Fehler.
Kiki findet	Deutsch gut.
Amadeus findet	Deutsch langweilig.
	die Fragen nicht.

A

1   What do you know about these people? The text *"Das ist meine Familie"* contains the information.

Name	Alter	Wohnort	Arbeit	Hobbys
Kurt	✕	Kaufungen		Video-Kamera Auto
Erika	✕			
Henning				
Großvater Großmutter			✕	
Monika				✕
Wencke				

2   Wenckes Familie.

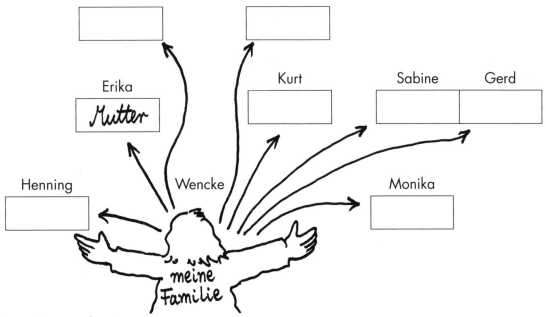

3   Learning word pairs.

Vater und   *Mutter*   Hund und   _____

Schwester und _____   interessant und   *langweilig*

Tante und   _____   _____

Großvater und _____   _____

Oma und   _____   _____

Cousin und   _____   _____

4 Wencke schreibt einen Brief an ihre neue Brieffreundin Julia in Rom. Julia liest den Brief, aber ...

Complete the missing parts of the letter.

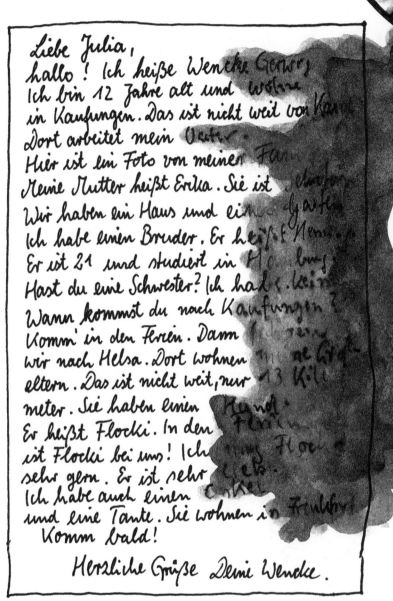

Liebe Julia,

hallo! Ich heiße Wencke Gerwer,
Ich bin 12 Jahre alt und wohne
in Kaufungen. Das ist nicht weit von Ka...
Dort arbeitet mein Vater.
Hier ist ein Foto von meiner Fam...
Meine Mutter heißt Erika. Sie ist ...
Wir haben ein Haus und eine...
Ich habe einen Bruder. Er heißt Henn...
Er ist 21 und studiert in Ha...
Hast du eine Schwester? Ich hab...
Wann kommst du nach Kaufungen?
Komm' in den Ferien. Dann ...
wir nach Helsa. Dort wohnen ... Groß-
eltern. Das ist nicht weit, nur 13 Kil...
meter. Sie haben einen Hund.
Er heißt Flocki. In den ...
ist Flocki bei uns! Ich ... Floc...
sehr gern. Er ist sehr ...
Ich habe auch einen Onkel
und eine Tante. Sie wohnen in Fra...
    Komm bald!

        Herzliche Grüße Deine Wencke.

5 Write your own letter.

6 Who is that? Listen to the cassette and write the names.

① _____
② _____
③ _____
④ _____
⑤ _____

Wencke

Henning   Sabine   Erika

Großvater

7   Listen to the cassette and draw the things being described.

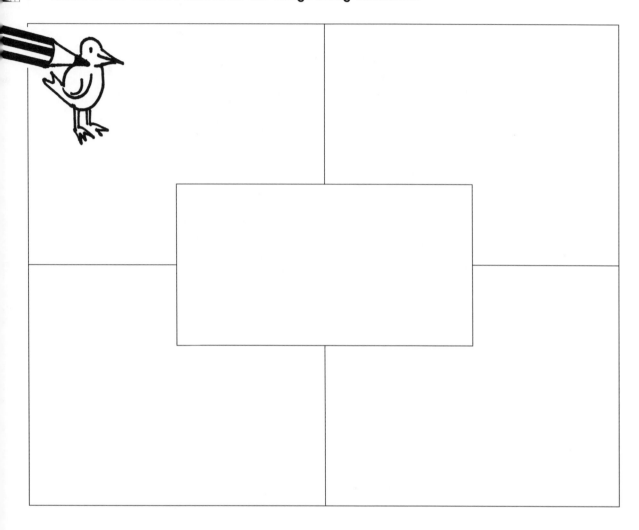

8   Fragen zu „Familie". How many questions can you write?

① _Wie heißt_ _____ ?

② _____ ?

③ _____ ?

④ _____ ?

⑤ _____ ?

⑥ _____ ?

⑦ _____ ?

⑧ _____ ?

A

1   Was weißt du von Graf Dracula? Write the words in the correct spaces.

Dracula ist _____.   sehr berühmt

Er ist auch _____.   in der Nacht

Er wohnt _____.   am Tag

Er hat _____.   ein großes Schloß

Er mag _____.   Musik

Er „arbeitet" _____.   in Transsylvanien

Er schläft _____.   sehr alt

2   Ein Gedicht über Dracula. Listen to the cassette and fill in the blanks.

Hört ihr, er ist wieder da,

Der berühmte _____!

Er lebt nicht in Portugal oder Spanien

Sondern in _____.

Dort hat er ein altes Schloß

Das ist sehr schön und auch sehr _____.

Er schläft von morgens früh um acht

Sechzehn Stunden bis _____.

Er war schon lange nicht mehr hier –

Doch heute nacht kommt er um _____!

B

3 **Ein Interview mit Heike.** Listen to the cassette a few times until you have filled in all the information.

	Was macht Heike?	Wann macht sie das?

Jeden Tag

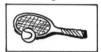

Heike steht auf.   *5 Minuten vor 7.*

_____   _____

Montag

_____

Dienstag

_____

Mittwoch

_____

Donnerstag

_____

Freitag

_____

Samstag

_____

Sonntag

_____

4 **Zeitansage im Radio.** Listen to the cassette and write down the times.

① _____ ② _____ ③ _____ ④ _____

⑤ _____ ⑥ _____ ⑦ _____ ⑧ _____

C

5 TIME ZONES · ZEITZONEN · FUSEAUX HORAIRES · FUSI ORARI

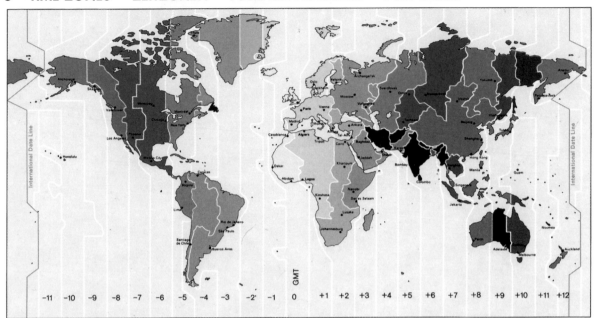

a In Frankfurt ist es 13 Uhr – in Jakarta ist es 19 Uhr: plus (+) 6 Stunden Differenz.
In Frankfurt ist es 13 Uhr – in New York ist es 7 Uhr: minus (–) 6 Stunden Differenz.

In Buenos Aires: 10 Uhr – in Teheran:_____

In New York: 24 Uhr – in Paris:_____

b In Tokio ist es Viertel vor 10. Wie spät ist es in Frankfurt? _____

In Paris ist es kurz nach 9. Wie spät ist es in London? _____

In Madrid ist es gleich 13 Uhr. Wie spät ist es in Bombay? _____

In Sydney ist es 14:56. Wie spät ist es in Oslo? _____

6 Comparing countries.

	Deutschland	mein Land
Wann beginnt der Unterricht?	oft um 7:45 Uhr oder um 8 Uhr	_____
Wann hört der Unterricht auf?	oft um 13 Uhr	_____
Wie lange dauert eine Schulstunde?	45 Minuten	_____
Wann gibt es Mittagessen?	von 12 bis 14 Uhr	_____
Wann gibt es Abendessen?	von 18 bis 20 Uhr	_____

A

1 Julia möchte mit Hannes schwimmen gehen. Sie ruft im Schwimmbad an. Höre zu und vergleiche die Öffnungszeiten. Frau Weber vom Schwimmbad sagt Julia die Öffnungszeiten. Eine Information ist falsch.

Schwimmbad Neckarhausen Öffnungszeiten

	geschlossen
Montag	8–11 Uhr
Dienstag	14–18 Uhr
	8–18 Uhr
Mittwoch	8 18 Uhr
Donnerstag	8–11 Uhr
Freitag	15–19 Uhr
	8–17 Uhr
Samstag	8–12 Uhr
Sonntag	

	Vormittag	Nachmittag
Montag	*geschlossen*	*geschlossen*
Dienstag	*8–11*	
Mittwoch		
Donnerstag		
Freitag		
Samstag		
Sonntag		

2 Julia ruft dann bei Hannes an. Höre das Gespräch von der Kassette. Was ist am Montag, Dienstag, Mittwoch, ...? What does Hannes tell Julia?

Montag	Dienstag	Mittwoch	Donnerstag	Freitag
Schwimmbad geschlossen	*Hannes hat am Nachmittag Schule und*			

Wann gehen Julia und Hannes schwimmen?   Am _____ um _____ Uhr.

B

3 Create your own language building blocks. Read the dialogs and then fill in the utterances in the correct tables.

- ● Wann gehen wir ins Kino?
- ○ Am Sonntag.
- ● Um 18 Uhr?
- ○ Nein, das geht nicht
- ● Um 20 Uhr 30?
- ○ Gut, einverstanden.

- ○ Kommst du am Freitag?
- ● Da kann ich nicht.
- ○ Dann komm am Samstag!
- ● Okay, wann?
- ○ Um 19 Uhr.

- ○ Gehen wir morgen schwimmen?
- ● Gute Idee!
- ○ Halb drei?
- ● Halb drei geht nicht. Geht halb vier auch?
- ○ Ja. Also halb vier.

? Fragen

Kommst du am Freitag?

_____

_____

+ Ja-sagen

Gut, einverstanden

_____

_____

− Nein-sagen

Nein, das geht nicht

_____

_____

4 Mit dem Dialogplan arbeiten.   Schreibe die Dialoge.

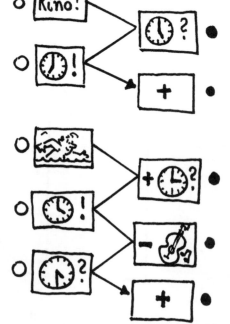

○ *Wir gehen ins Kino. Gehst du mit?*

● *Wann geht ihr? Um 5 Uhr?*

○ _____

● _____

○ *Wir gehen schwimmen. Kommst du mit?*

● *Wann geht ihr? Um 3 Uhr?*

○ _____

● _____

○ _____

● _____

C

5 Mark the stressed syllable.

<u>Mo</u>ntag   Dienstag   Mittwoch   Donnerstag   Freitag   Samstag

kombinieren   buchstabieren   korrigieren   Dialog   Konzert   Fußball   Katze   Telefon

vorlesen

6 Which sentence is marked for correct intonation?

a ① – Wann <u>gehen</u> wir ins Kino?
      – <u>Am</u> Samstag.

② – Wann gehen wir ins <u>Kino?</u>
      – Am <u>Samstag.</u>

b ① – Kommst du am <u>Donnerstag?</u>
      – Ja, um <u>halb neun.</u>

② – Kommst <u>du</u> am Donnerstag?
      – Ja, <u>um</u> halb neun.

c ① – Kommst <u>du</u> am Sonntag?
      – Nein, meine <u>Schwester.</u>

② – Kommst du am <u>Sonntag?</u>
      – Nein, <u>meine</u> Schwester.

d ① – Gehen wir am <u>Samstag</u> schwimmen?
      – Nein, am <u>Sonntag.</u>

② – Gehen <u>wir</u> am Samstag schwimmen?
      – Nein, <u>am</u> Sonntag.

e ① – Komm doch um <u>fünf!</u>
      – Geht es um halb sechs <u>auch?</u>
      – <u>O.k.,</u> halb <u>sechs.</u>

② – Komm <u>doch</u> um fünf!
      – <u>Geht</u> es um halb sechs auch?
      – O.k., <u>halb</u> sechs.

7 Listen carefully to the cassette and mark the stressed words in the sentence.

a ○ Gehst du heute abend mit ins Kino?
   ● Nein, ich habe Klavierstunde.

b ○ Kommst du mit? Wir spielen Fußball
   ● O.k., ich komme in zehn Minuten.

c ○ Gehst du morgen mit schwimmen?
   ● Wann geht ihr?
   ○ Um vier.
   ● Gut, ich gehe mit.

d ○ Was machst du heute abend?
   ● Ich mache nichts!
   ○ Gehst du mit ins Kino?
   ● Ich weiß nicht. Wann geht ihr?
   ○ Um sechs.
   ● O.k., da gehe ich mit.

A

1 Compound words.

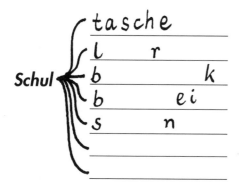

Schul- tasche
l   r
b   k
b   e i
s   n
_____
_____

Was ist in der Schultasche?

ein L _____

_____

_____

_____

_____

2 Which words belong together?

Lehrer-   -lehrerin
Physik-   -zimmer
            -stift
Sport-   -buch
Blei-   -halle
            -raum
Deutsch-   -unterricht
Stunden-   -plan

das Lehrerzimmer _____

_____

_____

_____

_____

3 Listen to the cassette. Draw a line from the door following the directions and then write the name of the room on the plan.

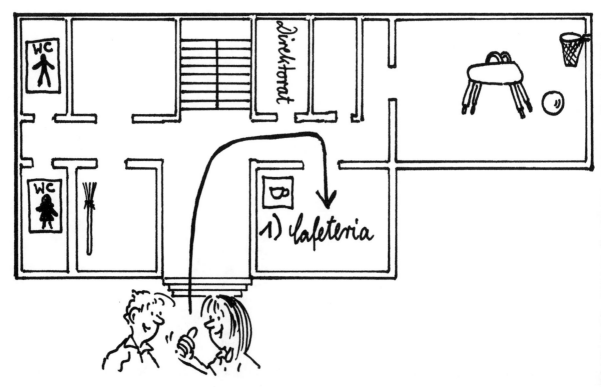

4 Read the text and draw the picture.

a Hier ist ein Haus.
  Es ist in der „Hauptstraße".
  Es hat die Nummer 4.
  Vor dem Haus ist ein Auto.
  Neben dem Haus steht ein Fahrrad.
  Über dem Haus fliegt ein Vogel.

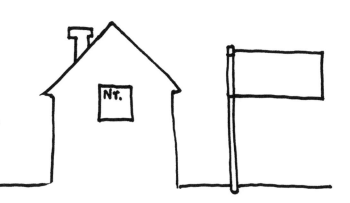

b Das ist Katja.
  Sie hat eine Brille.
  Sie hat ein Gebiß wie Dracula.
  Sie sitzt auf einem Stuhl.
  Unter dem Stuhl sitzt ihre Katze.
  Links neben dem Stuhl sitzt ihr Hund.

5 Schreibe die Fragen.

a _Wo ist bitte das Sekretariat_ ?   Das Sekretariat? Hier durch den Eingang rein, dann rechts.

b _____ ?   Jetzt ist es genau 5 Minuten vor 12.

c _____ ?   Der Unterricht beginnt 10 Minuten nach 8.

d _____ ?   Meine Freundin heißt Katja.

e _____ ?   Das ist ein Papagei.

f _____ ?   Klavierunterricht habe ich von 2 bis 4.

g _____ ?   Das sind 5 Hunde.

h _____ ?   Dracula kommt aus Transsylvanien.

6 Fill in the blanks. Check your answers with the cassette.

Sherlock Holmes, Watson und P. C. Chip

Es ist Mitternacht. Sherlock Holmes schläft
noch nicht!
Er ist in_____Stadt. Er sucht _____
Mann. _____ Mann heißt „P. C. Chip".
P. C. Chip mag Computer, Radios, Kassetten
und Schreibmaschinen. Sherlock Holmes hat
_____ Foto von P. C. Chip.
P. C. Chip hat _____ Brille und _____
Tasche. _____ Tasche ist sehr groß!
Jetzt sieht Sherlock Holmes P. C. Chip. Wohin
geht P. C. Chip um Mitternacht? Er geht
_____ Schule! In _____ Schule gibt es
viele Computer. P. C. Chip ist ein Computer-
experte. Und Sherlock Holmes geht mit – aber
P. C. Chip weiß es nicht! Jetzt ist P. C. Chip
vor _____ Schule, dann hinter _____
Schule. Er geht in _____ Schule, ganz lang-
sam! Wo ist _____ Hausmeister?? Er schläft!
Sherlock ist _____ Park, hinter der Schule.
Er paßt gut auf! Er hat ein Walkie-Talkie:
Er spricht jetzt mit Watson, seinem Freund:
„Hallo, Watson, hörst du mich?" – „Ja, wo bist
du?" – „Ich bin _____ Park, hinter _____
Schule. P. C. Chip ist jetzt in _____ Schule.
Jetzt ist er _____ Erdgeschoß, _____
Sekretariat." – „Und was macht er jetzt?" –
„Jetzt geht er _____ Treppe hoch, _____
Physikraum." – „Und jetzt?" – „Jetzt kommt
er wieder _____ Treppe runter." – „Hat er
die Computer?" – „Ich weiß nicht. Jetzt ist er
vor _____ Büro von Dr. Lindemann. Jetzt
kommt er _____ Ausgang. Jetzt ist er
_____ Park. Und jetzt habe ich ihn. –

HALT! SHERLOCK HOLMES!
HÄNDE HOCH!!

A

1   It's your birthday. Write an invitation to your friend. Use the hints on the right.

Liebe/r ... .
Am ... habe ich Geburtstag.
Ich lade Dich zu meiner Party ein.
Die Party beginnt um ... .
Hast du Zeit?
Dein/e ...

2   Write your friend a birthday card.

Liebe(r)

13

3 **Learning Tip** Learn these words together all in a row.

Frühling _____ _____ _____

Januar _____ _____ April _____ _____

Juli _____ _____ Oktober _____ _____

4 Was machst du ...

... im Sommer? **... im Winter?**

schwimme ich *laufe ich Ski*

_____ _____

_____ _____

_____ _____

_____ _____

_____ _____

_____ _____

_____ _____

_____ _____

_____ _____

_____ _____

_____ _____

Tennis spielen
Ski laufen
Basketball spielen
Freunde besuchen
Ferien machen
im Garten helfen
reiten
Fußball spielen
schwimmen
lesen
schlafen
Rad fahren
Musik machen

5 Jahreszeiten ...

... in Deutschland: **... in deinem Land:**

Winter {
Dezember
Januar
Februar

Winter: _____, _____, _____

Frühling {
März
April
Mai

Frühling: _____, _____, _____

Sommer {
Juni
Juli
August

Sommer: _____, _____, _____

Herbst {
September
Oktober
November

Herbst: _____, _____, _____

6 Listen and write down the dates on which the seasons begin in Germany.

Frühling: _____   Sommer: _____

Herbst: _____   Winter: _____

Wann beginnen die Jahreszeiten in deinem Land?

7 Listen and write down the dates you hear.

a _____   b _____   c _____

d _____   e _____   f _____

8 An overview of time.

199...

Das **Jahr** hat 4 _____:

Frühling, _____, _____, _____

und 12 _____:

_____, _____, _____, _____,

_____, _____, _____, _____,

_____, _____, _____, _____.

Ein **Monat** hat 4 _____

und 30 oder 31 _____.

Der Monat Februar hat 28 (oder 29) _____.

Eine **Woche** hat 7 _____:

Montag, _____, _____, _____,

_____, _____, _____.

Ein **Tag** hat 24 _____.

Tageszeiten: der Morgen, _____, _____, _____

_____, _____.

Tag und _____.

Eine **Stunde** hat 60 _____.

Eine **Minute** hat 60 _____.

A

1 Read the text and fill in the blanks.

Udo Lindenberg:
Eine Rock-Legende

Die Karriere von Udo Lindenberg (*1946) beginnt schon im Jahre 1959. Am Anfang war er Schlagzeuger in verschiedenen Jazz- und Rockgruppen. 1969 spielt er dann bei der Hamburger Gruppe „City Preachers" und gründet 1973 seine berühmte Band „Das Panik-Orchester".

„Das Panik-Orchester" war zwar nicht die erste deutsche Rockband mit deutschen Texten, aber Lindenbergs Songs machten die deutsche Sprache in der Rockmusik populär.

Lindenberg spricht die Sprache seiner Generation. In den 70er und 80er Jahren hatte er großen Erfolg mit Titeln wie „Alles klar auf der Andrea Doria", „Sister King Kong" und „Panische Zeiten". Seine Platten und CDs sind Klassiker der deutschen Rock-Szene.

„Das Panik-Orchester" gibt es seit ein paar Jahren nicht mehr. Udo Lindenberg gibt auch nicht mehr so viele Konzerte wie früher, und er macht keine Tourneen. Aber er hat immer wieder Erfolg mit neuen Liedern.

UDO L
Karriere beginnt _____*1959*_____

in: _____

1969: _____

1973: Das „_____"

Texte: _____

70er/80er JAHRE

Viele CDs und _____

_____

HEUTE

_____

viele Konzerte

keine _____

Aber: _____

mit neuen Liedern.

2 Was ist richtig? Was ist falsch?

	richtig	falsch
Udo Lindenberg spielt in seiner Band Gitarre.		x
Seine Karriere beginnt mit 13 Jahren.		
1969 war er Schlagzeuger bei der Gruppe „City Preachers".		
Seine Band war „Das Panik-Orchester".		
Er hatte großen Erfolg mit Texten in deutscher Sprache.		

3 Ergänze den Text.

Ein Rock-Star

Er heißt Udo _____. Er _____ aus Hamburg. Er ist

_____ Jahre alt. Er macht seit _____ Rock-_____. Seine Band war „Das

_____". Er hatte großen Erfolg mit Liedern in _____

Sprache. Er schreibt immer wieder neue _____.

4 Eine Pop-Sängerin.

NENA

Anfang der 80er Jahre hatte sie mit ihren Liedern internationalen Erfolg, z. B. mit dem Song „99 Luftballons". 1984 und 1985 war sie in Japan auf Tournee. Dann war eine lange Pause – bis 1993. Dann hatte sie wieder einen Hit mit „bongo girl".

A   This exercise is not easy. Can you fill in all the blanks?

a Nena ist _____.

b Mit dem Song „99 Luftballons" hatte sie _____.

c Bis 1993 war _____.

d Ihr neuer Titel _____.

B   This one is easy. Which of the following statements are correct?

richtig

a Nena spielt Schlagzeug und Gitarre. ❐

b Ihr Song „99 Luftballons" war ein großer Erfolg. ❐

c 1980–1990 war sie viel auf Tournee. ❐

d „bongo girl" – so heißt der neue Titel. ❐

B

5 „War" oder „hatte"? Ergänze die Sätze.

a Udo Lindenberg _____ Schlagzeuger.

b Er _____ großen Erfolg mit „Sister King Kong"

c Nena _____ mit Ihrem Lied „99 Luftballons" Erfolg.

d Das _____ in den 80er Jahren.

e 1984 und 1985 _____ Nena in Japan.

f Udo _____ zuerst bei der Gruppe „City Preachers", dann _____ er seine
eigene Band, „Das Panik-Orchester".

6 Rock Stars auf Tournee.

Rock Legends on Tour ✈

NENA
5.3. Braunschweig, 6.3. Beverungen,
8.3. Offenbach, 10.3. Saarbrücken,
11.3. Nürnberg, 12.3. Lichtenfels,
13.3. München, 14.3. Augsburg,
16.3. Köln, 17.3. Borken, 18.3. Berlin,
20.3. Chemnitz, 21.3. Stuttgart,
22.3. Halle, 24.3. Hamburg,
25.3. Hannover, 26.3. Hagen,
28.3. Mannheim

PAUL SIMON
20.6. München, 27.6. Berlin,
29.6. Hamburg, 3.7. Stuttgart,
4.7. Dortmund

URIA HEEP
13.4. Zürich, 14.4. Salzburg, 16.4. Linz,
17.4. Graz, 18.4. Wien,
23.4. München, 25.4. Erfurt, 29.4. Köln,
3.5. Berlin

STING
1.5. Berlin, 2.5. Kiel, 4.5. Dortmund,
13.5. München, 15.5. Stuttgart,
17.5. Frankfurt/Main

Beantworte die folgenden Fragen.

a An welchen Tagen macht NENA eine Pause?

_____

b Wann ist PAUL SIMON in Dortmund?

_____

c An welchen Tagen ist URIA HEEP

in der Schweiz? _____

in Österreich? _____

in Deutschland? _____

d Wann ist wer in Berlin?

PAUL SIMON: _____

URIA HEEP: _____

STING: _____

 7 Nena und Udo. Höre die Kassette.

Review exercises for Units 9–14

1 Was sagst du? Was fragst du?

1 **John ist neu in deiner Klasse.
Die Schüler fragen:**

a Name? _____

b Adresse/Straße? _____

c Hobbys? _____

d Haustier? _____

e Lieblingsfach? _____

f Musikinstrument? _____

g Sport? _____

2 **Here are the answers to the questions in Exercise 1. Match them up with the correct questions.**

① Ja, ich habe eine Katze.
② Ich spiele Klavier.
③ Ich heiße John Herkless.
④ Ich schwimme gerne.

⑤ Ich wohne jetzt in der Goethestraße 14.
⑥ Ich mag Sport.
⑦ Ich höre gerne Rockmusik.

1	2	3	4	5	6	7
d						

3 **Dialoge schreiben.**

Wann hast du Mathe? _____ (Montag/
9:45–10:30)

Dienstag auch? _____ (–)

Und am Mittwoch? _____ (8:55–9:40)

Magst du Mathe? _____ (–)

_____ (+)

Hast du ein
Lieblingsfach? _____ (+)

4 Write a dialog by putting the utterances in order.

Am Donnerstagnachmittag.

_____

Das geht nicht, da habe
ich Gitarrenunterricht.

_____

_____

Gehst du mit in den Zoo?
Die Elefanten haben ein Baby.

_____

Geht es am Sonntagvormittag?

_____

Ja gut, um 10.

_____

Ja, Sonntagvormittag ist o.k.

_____

Um 10 Uhr am Eingang?

_____

Wann?

_____

**5 Was sagen die Tiere?
Be creative.**

2 Wörter

6 Write the words in the correct columns.

Cousine · U̶h̶r̶ · Großmutter · S̶t̶u̶n̶d̶e̶ · Onkel · M̶o̶n̶a̶t̶ · Herbst · Tante · Sekunde · Tag · Morgen · Sohn · M̶a̶i̶ · Minute · Großvater · Februar · V̶a̶t̶e̶r̶ · Cousin · Mittag · M̶u̶t̶t̶e̶r̶ · Oma · Bruder · Opa · Schwester · Frühling · Abend · Mitternacht · Pause · T̶o̶c̶h̶t̶e̶r̶

♂ Familie ♀		🕐 Zeit	MAI
Vater	*Mutter*	*Uhr*	*Monat*
	Tochter	*Stunde*	*Mai*

7 Grammar – Language: List the words according to grammar functions.

das · A̶n̶t̶w̶o̶r̶t̶ · aufhören · die · er · Fahrrad · schreiben · der · unser · sie · mein · schlafen · ein · Wort · kein · Familie · sein · gehen · ihr · Japan

Nomen	Verben	Pronomen	Artikel
Antwort			

8 Do you remember these word pairs?

links und _____ _____ und heute

intelligent und _____ _____ und falsch

oben und _____ _____ und Schwester

groß und _____ _____ und Nacht

mein und _____ _____ und Frau

9 Find 11 music words and write them down.

K	A	F	T	A	N	G	U	M	M
H	I	R	N	E	T	A	L	U	F
F	A	N	P	H	O	R	N	S	G
A	S	T	L	E	U	K	B	I	I
N	L	O	R	N	R	O	C	K	T
S	I	N	G	E	N	N	R	E	A
L	I	E	D	B	E	Z	I	R	R
C	D	L	T	U	E	E	L	U	R
R	O	M	K	S	I	R	O	B	E
F	L	U	P	L	A	T	T	E	Q

CD _____

_____

_____

_____

_____

_____

_____

_____

_____

_____

10 Ergänze die Sätze.

Wieviel _____ ist es?   Zeit / Uhr / Stunde / Minute

Wo ist _____ Deutschbuch?   die / mein / sie / uns

Der Physikraum liegt neben der _____.   Turnhose / Cafeteria / Direktor

Unser Biolehrer hat einen _____.   Pferd / Esel / Katze / Kaninchen

11 Was machen die Leute?

_____

_____

_____

_____

12 Tageszeiten

der Mittag

die Nacht

der

der

13 Write out the numbers.

a Die Tournee beginnt am 21. 3. (einund_____ drit _____)

b Das Jahr beginnt am 1.1. (_____ _____)

c Die Ferien hören am 29. 8. auf (_____ _____)

d Weihnachten ist am 24.12. (_____ _____)

14 Combine the words to make new words that will fit in the sentences below.

Haus +

Meister   Auto

Nummer   Aufgabe   Artikel   Atlas

Tier   Bus   Cousin

a Unser _____ heißt Müller.

b Meine _____ ist 64.

c _____ mag ich nicht.

d John hat auch ein _____.

3 Intonation

15 Lang oder kurz: Höre zu und kreuze an.

	lang	kurz
Fach		✕
fahren		
falsch		
Fehler		
Fisch		

	lang	kurz
finden		
Frage		
Füller		
fünf		
Fuß		

16 Wortakzent: Markiere die betonte Silbe.

aussprechen   Automat   August   Antwort   April   Adresse

Abend   Artikel   Akzent   Affe   Alphabet   anders

Amadeus   Zeichnung   Zitrone   zusammenfassen

17 Listen to the cassette. Write a question mark in the boxes next to the words that are at the end of questions. Leave the others blank.

a …Zeit [?]   **c** …Oma [ ]   **e** …Papier [ ]   **g** …Diktat [ ]

b …Füller [ ]   **d** …Satz [ ]   **f** …Hund [ ]   **h** …7c [ ]

4 Spelling

18 20 schwere Wörter.

Study these words for three minutes and then turn to the next page and do Exercise 23.

Adresse · Ansichtskarte · aufpassen · chinesisch · buchstabieren · diskutieren · fair ·
Fahrrad · Frühling · Verabredung · wiederholen · Theater · studieren · Straßenbahn ·
Begrüßung · Herbstferien · zusammengehören · Glückwunsch · Ergänzung · Grammatik

5 Grammatik

19 First complete the table and then fill in the blanks.

ich	*mein*
du	_____
er/es	_____
sie	_____
wir	_____
ihr	_____
sie	_____

M_____ Hund heißt Waldi. Er ist drei Jahre alt.
M_____ Schwester hat eine Katze. I_____
Freundin hat zwei Kaninchen. I_____ Namen sind
Cäsar und Kleopatra. U_____ Mathelehrer hat einen
Esel. S_____ Name ist Murro. Er kommt aus Spanien.
Und du? Hat d_____ Mathelehrer auch ein Haustier?

20 Fill in the blanks with the correct two-part verb.

vor   schauen
                    lesen
an
        hören
auf
mit   kommen
zu   stehen

a _____ euch das Bild an.

b Peter _____ morgens um 8 Uhr auf.

c _____ du am Sonntag mit ins Kino?

d Martina, _____ bitte den Text vor.

e Ich lese jetzt einen Text vor. _____ bitte zu.

21 Can you change these verbs into nouns? Can you complete the Learning Tip?

üben	*die Übung*	betonen	_____
wiederholen	_____	zeichnen	_____
verabreden	_____	begrüßen	_____

Learning Tip ▷ Nomen mit „-ung", Artikel immer „_____"

6 Lesen

22 Drei Briefe.

a Put the two parts of each letter together.
b Match the letters with the correct pictures.

Ⓐ ◯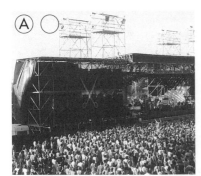

Ⓑ ◯

Ⓒ ◯

① Liebe Nilgün,
gestern war ich im Metallica-Konzert.
Die Band war wirklich super, besonders
Marco. Er spielt ganz toll Gitarre.

④ Um 6 war das Programm vorbei. Dann
waren wir noch einen Hamburger essen.
Tschüs
Dein Jochen

② Hallo Sandra,
am Wochenende war ich im Zirkus.
Das Programm war Spitze!
Elefanten, Tiger und Artisten.
Aber die Clowns waren ein bißchen
langweilig.

⑤ Der Campingplatz war sehr
komfortabel. Jetzt beginnt die Schule
wieder. Das ist blöd.
Viele Grüße
Dein Ralf

③ Lieber Udo,
die Sommerferien waren wirklich toll. Wir
waren am Bodensee. Wir hatten zwei
Wochen Sonne! Wir hatten
Fahrräder und waren in Österreich und
in der Schweiz.

⑥ Sie machen jetzt eine Tournee. Nächstes
Wochenende sind sie bei Euch in Zürich.
Gehst du hin?
Alles Gute und liebe Grüße
Deine Renja

1 + _____   2 + _____   3 + _____

23 Complete the words from exercise 18.

Adre_____   Ansi_____karte   aufp_____en

chine_____ch   buc_____eren   dis_____ren

fai_____   Fah_____ad   Früh_____g

Verab_____g   wie_____olen   Thea_____

stud_____n   Straße_____ahn   Begr_____ung

Herb_____erien   zusam_____hören   Glück_____sch

Erg_____zung   Gr_____tik.

A

1 Don't look in the text. Was ist auf dem Partytisch auf Seite 78 im Kursbuch?

① Mineralwasser ☐   ⑦ Katze ☐   ⑬ Bier ☐   ⑲ Salat ☐

② Atlas ☐   ⑧ Banane ☐   ⑭ Elefant ☐   ⑳ Pizza ☐

③ Affe ☐   ⑨ Füller ☐   ⑮ Pommes frites ☐   ㉑ Ei ☐

④ Cola ☐   ⑩ Schokolade ☐   ⑯ Würstchen ☐   ㉒ Käse ☐

⑤ Buch ☐   ⑪ Apfelsaft ☐   ⑰ Giraffe ☐   ㉓ Fisch ☐

⑥ Kuli ☐   ⑫ Bleistift ☐   ⑱ Radiergummi ☐   ㉔ Limonade ☐

Put the remaining words in three groups.

B

2 Sechs Wörter passen zu Party. Welche?

Spiel · Einladung · Schule · Problem ·
tanzen · Musik · Lehrerin · trinken ·
Wörterbuch · essen · Hausmeister ·
Kaninchen

Party

3 Welche Wörter passen zusammen?

Gitarre · Comic · Fotos · Kuchen · Videos · Cola · Lied · Moped · Spaß · Freunde · Party	ansehen · essen · trinken · singen · machen · schreiben · lernen · spielen · lesen · haben · treffen · vorlesen

Musik + hören, machen
Fotos +

4 Einladungsbrief

Iris macht eine Geburtstagsparty. Sie schreibt eine Einladung an ihre Freundin Sabrina. Write an invitation using the phrases below.

> Liebe Sabrina,
> nächsten Samstag feiere ich meinen Geburtstag.
> 1 Tschüs, Deine Iris.
> 2 Dazu lade ich Dich herzlich ein.
> 3 Bitte antworte bald.
> 4 Um 11 Uhr hören wir auf.
> 5 Klaus, Dieter, Marco, Claudia, Sabine und Stefanie kommen auch.
> 6 Zuerst machen wir Spiele.
> 7 Die Party beginnt um sechs Uhr.
> 8 Dann tanzen wir.

5 Was verstehst du?

**Du bist auf einer Party in
Deutschland. Die Leute reden.
Die Musik ist sehr laut. Was
verstehst du? Über welche
Themen reden die Leute?**

Diese Wörter verstehe ich:

① _____

_____

_____

Thema:

② _____

_____

_____

Thema:

6 Geburtstagspartys in Deutschland – Ergänze den Text.

Viele Ju _____ feiern P_____ mit Freunden und _____ innen

aus der Kla _____. Die P_____ beginnen meistens schon am _____mittag, um

15 _____. Es gibt Kuchen und C_____. Am liebsten essen alle Würst _____

oder H _____ mit Pommes frites. Die _____ und Mädchen spielen

Fuß _____, Karten oder sehen V_____. _____ 20 oder 21 Uhr _____ alle

nach _____.

7 Schreibe eine Einladungskarte zu deinem Geburtstag.

Du feierst Geburtstag.
Du feierst zu Hause.
Du feierst am Montag.
Du feierst von 16–19 Uhr.

Liebe (r) _____

_____

_____

D

R 8   Komparative – Superlative. Fülle die Tabelle aus.

a	**ä**	**ä**
stark	stärker	am stärksten
lang	_____	_____
alt	_____	am ältesten

o	**ö**	**ö**
groß	_____	_____
hoch	höher	_____

u	**ü**	**ü**
dumm	_____	_____
jung	_____	_____

viel

mehr
am meisten

gut

_____

_____

gern

_____

_____

9   Use your text to find the information.

Kiki
Amadeus   … ist größer/älter … als …
Wencke   … hat mehr … als …
Fredo   … mag … nicht so gern wie …
Klaus   … mag … lieber als …
Anja   … ist nicht so groß/alt wie …
Heike

B

1 Ergänze die Sätze.

> eine Party · mein Deutschbuch · von Amadeus · heute wieder ganz viel · den ganzen Nachmittag · drei Stunden · mit seinem Hund · noch keine Wörter · die Schule

a Ich habe _____ gelernt.

b Die Party hat _____ gedauert.

c Daniel hat _____ gespielt.

d Letzte Nacht habe ich _____ geträumt.

e Um 13 Uhr hat _____ aufgehört.

f Zwei Stunden habe ich _____ gesucht.

g Für den Mathetest habe ich _____ geübt.

h Letzten Samstag hat Christine_____ gemacht.

i Unsere Lehrerin hat _____ geredet.

2 Ergänze die Sätze und kontrolliere mit der Kassette.

> aufpassen · wiederholen · produzieren · zuhören · buchstabieren · träumen · machen · wiederholen · korrigieren · lernen · fragen · sagen

a Gestern haben wir im Deutschunterricht Wörter wieder _____ t.

b Klaus hat nicht auf _____ t und viele Fehler pro _____ t.

c Die Lehrerin hat das Wort „LEXIKON" b _____ t: L E X I K O N.

d Klaus hat gerade von Kiki ge _____ t und deshalb nicht zu _____ t.

e Er hat aus dem Wort „Lexikon" ein neues Wort ge _____ t: „Lesicon".

f Die Lehrerin hat ihn k _____ t: „Lexikon". Klaus hat das Wort

w_____t:

g L E X I K O N. „Richtig", hat die Lehrerin g_____., „jetzt hast du schon wieder

ein Wort richtig g _____ t!"

h Nach fünf Minuten hat die Lehrerin Klaus ge _____ t: „Wie heißt das neue

Wort?" – „Wörterbuch", war die Antwort von Klaus!

3 Hier ist eine Liste mit Partizip-II-Formen. Schreibe dazu das Verb im Infinitiv.
Use the verbs and forms of *haben* to complete the sentences.

angeschaut	*anschauen*
gearbeitet	
aufgepaßt	
besucht	
diskutiert	
gehabt	
gehört	

Heute habe ich einen Film **angeschaut**.

Gestern _____ ich 3 Stunden im Garten _____.

Du _____ im Unterricht nicht _____, oder?

Am Sonntag _____ wir den Zoo _____.

_____ ihr schon einmal in der Schule über Politik _____?

Wie lange _____ ihr Sommerferien _____?

_____ du schon die neue CD von „Chico" _____?

korrigiert	*korrigieren*
gelebt	
gelernt	
gemacht	
geordnet	
geredet	

DIKTAT? …
Hast du schon das Diktat korrigiert?

DRACULA/TRANSSYLVANIEN …

DIE NEUEN WÖRTER? …

HAUSAUFGABEN? …

WÖRTER/NACH DEM ALPHABET? …

AUF DER PARTY/NICHT GETANZT, NUR …

Now write your own sentences.

geträumt	
geübt	
vorgespielt	
wiederholt	
zugehört	
zugeordnet	

Ich habe

*Ich habe heute nichts versäumt,
denn ich hab nur von dir geträumt…*

4 Fragen im Perfekt. Was paßt zusammen?

die Lücken im Text	korrigieren
das Diktat	machen
die Hausaufgaben	markieren
die Endungen	ordnen
die Sätze	üben
das Lied	vorspielen
die Wörter	kombinieren
die Kassette	hören
die Grammatik	ergänzen

Hast du die Lücken im Text ergänzt?

5 Sätze bauen. Hier sind 25 Wörter. Make four sentences. Schreibe sie in dein Heft.

Party · hat · haben · auch · gemacht · am · Freitag · Sie · und · Musik · Sie · gehört · gekocht · Stunden · eine · zusammen · Sie · Die · gedauert · haben · Sie · haben · getanzt · vier · Schüler · Spaghetti

6 Sherlock Holmes macht ein Interview mit PC Chip. Höre das Interview und ergänze den Text.

> gespielt · war · war · gegangen · gegangen · mitgenommen · gelernt · gezeigt · gegessen · getrunken · geschrieben · gemacht · diskutiert · repariert

● Was haben Sie in der Schule gemacht, Herr Chip?

○ Ich _____ meinen Freund Rolf Meister besucht, er ist Hausmeister. Zuerst haben wir
Tischtennis _____, dann haben wir Abendessen _____. Wir
haben Spaghetti mit Ketchup _____ und Cola _____. Dann
sind wir durch die Schule _____. Rolf hat mir die PCs _____.
Wir haben über Computerprogramme _____. Das _____ sehr interessant.
Ich habe viel _____ und viel in mein Heft _____. Ein PC _____
kaputt. Ich bin nach Hause _____ und habe den PC _____.
Zu Hause habe ich den PC _____. Jetzt ist er wieder o.k. Hier ist er. Kein
Problem, oder?

B

1 Nadine fragt nach dem Weg.
Höre das Gespräch zwischen
Nadine und der Frau.
Kreuze an.

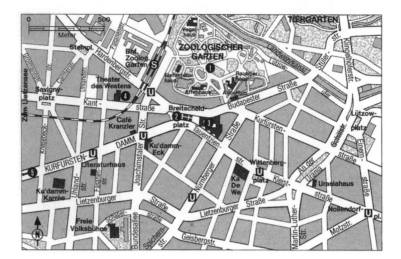

a **Wohin will Nadine?**
Zum „Bahnhof Zoo"
Zum Bahnhof
Zum „Hotel am Zoo"

b **Sie kommt zur Kantstraße.
Wohin muß sie gehen?**
rechts
links

2 **Im Kursbuch Seite 88 findest du den Stadtplan von Eisenach. Start at the Info in
Bahnhofstraße.**
a Eine Frau fragt dich: „Wie komme ich zum Lutherhaus."
b Ein junger Mann fragt: „Wie komme ich zum Bachhaus?"

Put the directions in order.

a „Wie komme ich zum Lutherhaus?"

Geradeaus sehen Sie das Lutherhaus. Gehen Sie dann über den Markt und dann nach
links. Dann durch das Nikolaitor und an der Nikolaikirche vorbei. Gehen Sie hier die
Bahnhofstraße entlang. Dann die Alexanderstraße entlang bis zum Markt.

b „Wie komme ich zum Bachhaus?"

Dann sehen Sie das Bachhaus auf der linken Seite. Also zuerst die Bahnhofstraße entlang.
Links ist der Stadtpark. Dann geradeaus. Vor dem Nikolaitor nach links. Gehen Sie über
den Frauenplan und dann geradeaus. Dann rechts in die Grimmelgasse bis zum Frauenplan. Dann die Wartburgallee entlang.

3 **In der Stadt – Satzintonation. Höre gut zu. Markiere die betonten Wörter.**

a Wie komme ich zur Wittenbergstraße?

b Wo ist denn hier der Bahnhof?

c Entschuldigung, ich suche die Goethestraße.

d ○ Können Sie mir sagen, wo das Rathaus ist?

   ● Hier immer geradeaus. Zweite Straße rechts.

e Tut mir leid, das weiß ich auch nicht.

f Immer geradeaus bis zur Ampel, dann links, dann die erste Straße rechts.

4 **Mirko, Bernd und Lumpi gehen in Düsseldorf spazieren.**

Am Burgplatz machen sie eine Pause.
Mirko hat eine Idee. Er sagt zu Bernd:
„Paß auf, wir machen jetzt ein Spiel. Ich
gehe los, und ihr wartet hier 10 Minuten.
Dann geht ihr auch los und sucht mich.
Lumpi hat eine sehr gute Nase, was
Lumpi!? Ihr könnt meinen Weg leicht
finden."

**Höre die Kassette und zeichne den
Weg von Mirko und von Bernd und
Lumpi durch Düsseldorf auf dem
Stadtplan ein. Was sieht Lumpi?
Begin at Burgplatz. Draw the route.**

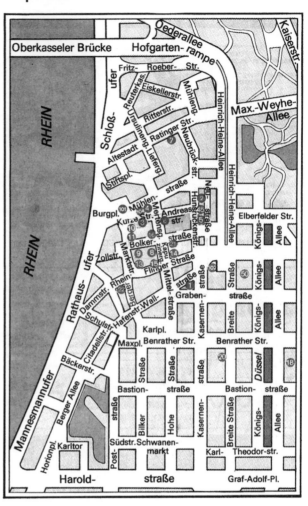

5 **Der ...-platz, die ...-straße, das ...-tor, die ...allee, das ...-ufer
Schreibe Beispiele aus dem Stadtplan auf.**

Der	... platz (pl.):	*der Karlplatz*
Die	... straße (str.):	_____
Das	... tor:	_____
Die	... allee:	_____
Das	... ufer:	_____

6 **Ich suche den Burgplatz. Höre die Kassette. Schreibe die Namen der Straßen,
Plätze ... auf und suche den Weg auf dem Stadtplan.**

Horionplatz

_____

_____

7 Klassenfahrt nach Eisenach

SHAWNEE MISSION SOUTH HIGH SCHOOL
Shawnee Mission Public Schools
5800 W. 107th St
Shawnee Mission, Kansas 66207
Telephone 913-967-7700

Educating for Life

Sehr geehrte Damen und Herren:

Wir sind die Klasse 9 an der Shawnee Mission South High School,
in Kansas in den USA. Im Februar machen wir eine Klassenexkursion
nach Deutschland. Wir planen auch einen Tag in Eisenach. Geben
Sie uns bitte ein paar Tips. Wir wissen nicht viel über Eisenach.

Haben Sie Informationsmaterial fuer uns? Bitte antworten Sie bald!

Eisenach
Information

Liebe Schüler der Klasse 9!

Vielen Dank für Euren Brief. Wir finden: Eine Exkursion nach Eisenach ist eine gute Idee.
Eisenach liegt in der Mitte von Deutschland. Die Stadt ist über 800 Jahre alt und sehr schön.
Wir haben viele schöne interessante Häuser im Zentrum. Kennt ihr Johann Sebastian Bach?
Er war ein Musiker und Komponist im 17. Jahrhundert. Er hat in Eisenach gelebt und gear-
beitet. Das Haus von Familie Bach ist jetzt ein Museum für interessante Musikinstrumente.
Auch Martin Luther hat hier gelebt. Er hat hier 3 Jahre die Schule besucht. Er hat die Bibel
ins Deutsche übersetzt. Nach Eisenach kommen viele Touristen. Alle besuchen die Wartburg.
Die Burg ist so alt wie die Stadt und eine internationale Touristenattraktion.
Aber Eisenach ist nicht nur historisch interessant. Die Autoindustrie von Eisenach hat eine
lange Tradition. Die „Wartburg"-Autos stehen im Automobilmuseum. Heute produzieren hier
BMW und OPEL.
In der Stadt gibt es zwei Jugendherbergen und ein Jugendzentrum. Wir organisieren auch
Exkursionen speziell für Jugendgruppen. Also, kommt nach Eisenach!

Match information and photographs.

A

1 **Kein Glück gehabt!**

**Lies den Text, und schreibe
die richtigen Verben aus dem
Kasten in die Lücken.
Höre dann die Kassette und
kontrolliere.**

zurückgehen   anziehen   sehen   essen

warten   sehen   kaufen

sein   weitergehen   trinken   sagen

Am Montag waren Karen und Silke auf dem Stadtfest. Es war sehr kalt und sie haben

zuerst einen Tee ___*getrunken*___ . Dann hatten sie richtig Hunger. Sie haben zwei

Hamburger _____. Aber die Hamburger waren schon kalt. Dann haben sie

einen Stand mit T-Shirts _____. „Toll, die neuen Kevin-Costner-T-Shirts!"

Aber nicht billig! 35 Mark! Na, ja, sie haben die T-Shirts _____. „Sie sind

ein bißchen groß", hat Karen _____. „Kein Problem! Die T-Shirts sind

ganz neu. Die müssen wir haben!". Sie haben die T-Shirts _____. Karen

und Silke haben viele interessante Jungen _____. Aber alle sind

_____. Heute war nicht ihr Tag. Sie sind zum Bus _____.

Sie haben 50 Minuten auf den Bus _____. Im Bus waren Heike und

Monika. Oh nein! Sie haben auch Kevin-Costner-T-Shirts gehabt. 10 Mark pro T-Shirt.

So ein Mist! Heute _____ nicht ihr Tag.

B

2 **Infinitiv oder Partizip II?**
Höre die Kassette und schreibe die Wörter in die richtige Liste.

Infinitiv	Partizip II
_____	_____
_____	_____
_____	_____

3 **Perfekt mit *sein* oder mit *haben*?**
**Kreuze zuerst an, höre dann die Kassette
und kontrolliere deine Lösung.**

	sein	haben
gehen		
kaufen		
kommen		
fragen		
sagen		
essen		
laufen		

4 Die Klassenfahrt – Sieh dir die Bilder an. Put the story in order.

○ Jedes Jahr macht die Klasse 8 a eine Klassenfahrt. Im letzten Jahr war die Klasse mit ihrer Lehrerin, Frau Seifert, in Eisenach. Sie haben die Wartburg besucht.

○ Der Herbergsvater hat sie begrüßt und ihnen die Jugendherberge und ihre Zimmer gezeigt. Schon bald hat es Mittagessen gegeben: Würstchen mit Pommes frites. Und für jeden Schüler eine Cola!

○ In diesem Jahr wollen die Schüler nicht in eine Stadt fahren. Sie haben lange diskutiert. Herr Knapp, der Klassenlehrer, hat eine Idee: „Es gibt eine Jugendherberge im Wald, nicht weit von hier. Sie heißt: Naturfreundehaus am Steinberg." Eine gute Idee! Und nur eine halbe Stunde mit dem Bus.

○ Beim Abendessen hat Herr Knapp gesagt: „Heute um 11 Uhr machen wir noch eine Wanderung durch den Wald! Vielleicht sehen wir um Mitternacht Dracula!"
Sie sind dann um 11 Uhr in den Wald gegangen. Es war ganz dunkel, uhuhuu! Sie waren ganz still, es war phantastisch! Aber Dracula haben sie nicht gesehen. Lange nach Mitternacht waren sie endlich im Bett.

○ Am Freitagmorgen haben sie sich vor der Schule getroffen. Um 10 Uhr ist dann der Bus gekommen. Er hat sie zum Naturfreundehaus am Steinberg gebracht.

○ Am Nachmittag haben sie nicht viel gemacht. Sie haben Tischtennis und Fußball gespielt.

5 Amadeus hat eine große Reise gemacht.

Amadeus war in der Schweiz, in Österreich, und er ist durch ganz Deutschland gefahren.
Jetzt ist er wieder zu Hause.

Kiki fragt:

Wo bist du gewesen?
Was hast du gesehen?
Was hast du gemacht?
Was war am interessantesten?
Was war am schönsten?
Hast du mir etwas mitgebracht?

Amadeus antwortet:

Ich war in München, in ...

**Write Amadeus' answers in your notebook.
Es gibt verschiedene Möglichkeiten.**

A

Bevor du die Übungen auf dieser Seite machst, sieh dir noch einmal die Grammatiktabellen auf Seite 122 hier im Arbeitsbuch an.

1 Was darf man, was muß man, was kann man in der Schule – was nicht?

Man darf	aufpassen.
Man muß	in die Bibliothek gehen und lesen.
Man darf nicht	keinen Elefanten mitbringen.
Man muß	den Lehrer fragen.
Man kann	im Deutschunterricht keinen Krimi lesen.
Man darf	die Schulsachen mitbringen.
Man kann	zu spät kommen.

2 Darfst du laute Musik hören? Höre die Kassette und kreuze an.

Ja   Nein

Muß Daniel um 9 Uhr ins Bett gehen?
Darf er am Wochenende bis 12 Uhr aufbleiben?
Der Vater liest – darf Naki dann Musik laut spielen?
Daniels Mutter ist Lehrerin. Sie korrigiert Hefte – muß
Daniel dann die Musik in seinem Zimmer leiser stellen?

B

3 Was sagen die Verkehrszeichen?

a müssen

 vorsichtig sein

Hier muß man vorsichtig sein.

 nach rechts fahren

Du _____

b nicht dürfen

 nicht halten

Ich _____

 nicht schneller als 60 fahren

Hier _____

c dürfen

 parken

Man _____

 über die Straße gehen

Wir _____

d können

_____

_____

4 Modalverben sammeln und ordnen.

Herr Direktor, dürfen wir heute nach der Pause nach Hause gehen?
Könnt ihr 10 Wörter ohne Fehler schreiben?
Kannst du mir bitte helfen? Ich verstehe die Aufgabe nicht.
Was ist los? – Wir können nicht ins Haus. Die Tür ist zu!
Wir müssen für Englisch 50 neue Wörter lernen.
Dürft ihr heute mit ins Kino gehen? – Nein, das geht nicht.
Herr Lehrer, darf ich Sie mal etwas fragen?
Müssen in Deutschland die Kinder eine Schuluniform tragen?
Wie lange mußt du noch zur Schule gehen?
Mein Papagei kann schon sehr gut Englisch, aber er muß noch Deutsch lernen.
Daniel und Naki dürfen am Samstag bis 11 Uhr aufbleiben. Am Sonntag können sie dafür lange schlafen.
Ich habe Hunger, ich muß unbedingt einen Hamburger essen.
Wencke darf mit zur Party gehen.
Darfst du schon Moped fahren? – Nein, ich bin noch nicht alt genug.
Sprich bitte etwas lauter. Ich kann dich nicht verstehen!
Müßt ihr im Unterricht immer reden?

	müssen	können	dürfen
ich			
du			
er/sie/es			
wir			
ihr			
sie			

5   Schreibe die Sätze richtig in die „Schraubzwinge" ein.

a   **Modalverben:**

Kannst du   _mir einen Bleistift_   _geben?_

Kannst du im Atlas Deutschland finden? Ich muß jeden Tag 3 Stunden Hausaufgaben machen. Möchtest du zu meiner Geburtstagsparty kommen? Darf man einen Hund in die Schule mitbringen?

b   **Perfekt:**

Hast du   _schon einmal Dracula_   _gesehen?_

Ich bin gestern 3 Kilometer gelaufen. Seid ihr gestern abend ins Kino gegangen? Bist du schon einmal in Berlin gewesen? Hast du dein Fahrrad schon repariert?

c   **Imperativ:**

Hör   _mir bitte eine Minute_   _zu!_

Ruf mich doch heute abend mal an! Paßt jetzt bitte ganz genau auf! Zieh doch das neue T-Shirt an! Schlage die Wörter im Wörterbuch nach!

d   **Trennbare Verben:**

Wencke steht   _jeden Tag um 7 Uhr_   _auf._

Schaust du den Film auch an? Wir passen gut zusammen. Spielst du mir das Lied noch einmal vor? Spreche ich das Wort richtig aus?

B

1 **Eine prima Suppe. Wie hast du die gemacht? –
Lies den Text. Write the recipe in your
notebook.**

Miriam hat ihren Freund Peter zum
Abendessen eingeladen. Sie hat Kartoffelsuppe
gekocht. Peter probiert die Suppe, dann ißt er
vier Teller Suppe! „Das schmeckt ja ganz
phantastisch!" sagt er. „Wie hast du das
gemacht?"

„Das ist nicht schwer", sagt Miriam. „Zuerst habe ich ein Pfund Kartoffeln und drei Möhren
geschält und gewaschen und in kleine Stücke geschnitten. Dann habe ich 100 Gramm
Speck und zwei Zwiebeln klein geschnitten und in einem großen Topf angebraten. Dazu
habe ich etwas Butter genommen.
Dann habe ich einen Liter Wasser dazugegeben und zum Kochen gebracht, dann die Kartoffeln und die Möhren dazugegeben und dazu ein bißchen Salz und Pfeffer. Das hat dann
ungefähr eine halbe Stunde gekocht. Zum Schluß habe ich noch zwei Löffel saure Sahne
dazugetan. Fertig!"

Was braucht man	Wie macht man das?
500 Gramm Kartoffeln	Zuerst die Kartoffeln und die Möhren schälen und waschen. Dann … Danach … Dann … Zum Schluß …

C

2 **Ein Interview mit vier Schülern.**

a **Express-Strategie beim Hören:**

Was ist das Thema in diesen Interviews? Kreuze an:

① Schule   ② Essen   ③ Freizeit   ④ Einkaufen

b **Schnüffel-Strategie beim Hören:**

Was ist richtig? Kreuze an.
① ☐ Peter mag Brezeln mit Butter.
② ☐ Jens frühstückt in der Schule.
③ ☐ Birgit muß schon im Unterricht essen.
④ ☐ Karin mag am liebsten Müsli.

c **Detektiv-Strategie beim Hören:**

Wer ist das?

Kiosk – Pause – Cola – Brezeln – Süßes

_____

3 Lesen
Bitte zuerst die Aufgaben lesen.

A Alle staunen, als der Zeppelin – voll mit Heliumgas – durch die Zentralhalle fliegt. Kleine Elektromotoren treiben ihn an. Ein Schüler lenkt ihn mit einer Funk-Fernsteuerung. Er ist das „kleinste Luftschiff" der Welt und kommt ins „Guinness-Buch der Rekorde".

B Aber von wegen! Tina hat ein neues Album und eine neue Single („I Don't Wanna Fight" – auf deutsch: Ich will nicht kämpfen) herausgebracht – und wird bei vier großen Open-Air-Festivals auf der Bühne stehen! Außerdem in diesem Jahr: Ein Kinofilm über Leben und Karriere der 53jährigen (!) „Rock-Oma", die – wie ihr

C her schlägt. Sie alle zusammen, die „Monsters Of Rock", sollen in einem Super-Festival zusammentreffen. Die größten Hardrock-Stars auf der größten Bühne, die jemals in Europa stand: 58 Meter breit, 26 Meter tief und 30 Meter hoch.

D **21.7.1969**
Der erste Mensch auf dem Mond! Der amerikanische Apollo-11-Austronaut Neil Armstrong betritt um 3.56 Uhr (MEZ) die Mondoberfläche. 500 Millionen Fernsehzuschauer in aller Welt sind live am Bildschirm dabei.

E Wasser zum Kochen bringen, Teebeutel in einer großen Kanne aufbrühen und 10 Minuten ziehen lassen. Tee mit Zucker süßen und kalt werden lassen. Dann die Zitronen auspressen, den Saft in den Tee geben und umrühren. Tee noch eine halbe Stunde in den Kühlschrank. Mit Eiswürfeln zusammen ins Glas füllen.

F Auto Union AG, der Konstrukteur war Ferdinand Porsche. Die Maximalleistung des Motors betrug 295 PS. Der Wagen hatte einen Sechzehnzylinder-Motor, hatte aber trotzdem nur ein Gewicht von 1090 kg. Mit diesem Typ A der Auto Union konnte die Höchstgeschwindigkeit von 280 km/h erreicht werden. Erfolg-

G Die Winterspiele in Albertville, dann Barcelona, aber zuvor, in diesem Monat, EURO 92: Das Endturnier der Fußball-Europameisterschaft in Schweden, vom 10. bis 26. Juni. Deutschland spielt in der Gruppe 2: Holland, Schottland, GUS. Gruppe 1: Schweden, Frankreich, Jugoslawien und England. Wir stellen hier die deutschen Asse in Bild und

a Themen und Texte: Write the letter of the texts that match the topics.

_____Essen   _____Sport   _____Musik

_____Schule   _____Technik   _____Tiere

b Typical words for each topic:

A _____

_____

B _____

_____

C _____

_____

D _____

_____

E _____

_____

F _____

_____

G _____

_____

Was sagst du? Was fragst du?

1 Ergänze die Fragen.

Dein Freund macht eine Party. Du fragst:

a Was _____?

b Wann _____?

c Wo _____?

d Wer _____?

e Wie lange _____?

2 Hier sind die Antworten zu Aufgabe 1. Ordne sie zu.

a Am Samstagnachmittag.
b Wencke, Jens, Hermann, Gabi, Monika und Michael.
c Von 17 bis 22 Uhr.
d Ich habe Geburtstag.
e Bei mir zu Hause.

3 Einen Dialog schreiben.

○ Wir müssen für die Party noch einkaufen.

● Was brauchen wir?

○ _____

● _____

○ Nein, wir haben noch drei Flaschen zu Hause.

● _____

○ Wir haben 30 Mark. Das ist genug!

● Was brauchen wir noch?

○ _____

● _____

○ Klar! Wir haben jede Menge Kassetten und CDs.

4 Ordne die Dialoge und schreibe sie ins Heft. Die Zeichnungen können helfen.

○ Bis Mittag habe ich geschlafen.

○ Ja, ganz prima! Am besten macht er Pizza.

○ Dann habe ich mir Spaghetti mit Ketchup gemacht.

● Kann dein Bruder kochen?

○ Er kann sehr gut Hamburger machen.

● Was hast du denn gestern gemacht?

● Und dann?

● Spitze! Das ist mein Lieblingsessen! Und was kann er noch?

● Phantastisch! Hamburger mag ich auch!

Wörter

5 Ordne die Wörter in zwei Gruppen. Wie heißen die Gruppen? Zwei Wörter passen nicht!

Rathaus · Kartoffel · Burg · Banane ·
Straße · Schokolade · Orange · Vater ·
Bahnhof · Stadtplan · Pizza · Salat ·
Ampel · Jugendherberge · Hamburger ·
Bleistift · Post · Eiscreme ·
Fußgängerzone · Salz · Kirche ·
Theater · Käse · Kuchen

6 Komposita bilden – Ergänze die passenden Wörter.

a Wo ist der Marktplatz? Hast du einen _____ plan?

b Das schmeckt gut. Ist das _____ auflauf?

c Müssen die Kinder in Deutschland eine _____ uniform tragen?

d Wie lange dauern in Deutschland die _____ ferien?

e Ist das ein _____ ballon? Kann der fliegen?

f Schlafen wir heute abend in der _____ herberge?

7 Welche Wörter passen zusammen?

Bus	Stuhl
Tisch	Esel
Hund	Moped
Fahrrad	Antwort
Frage	Katze
Pferd	Straßenbahn

_____

_____

_____

_____

_____

8 Ein Rätsel: A ist ein Teil von B.

A
Buch
Sonntag
Minute
Dezember
Pizza
Perfekt
Berlin
Lied
Fußball

B
Stunde
Musik
Sport
Deutschland
Grammatik
Essen
Jahr
Woche
Bibliothek

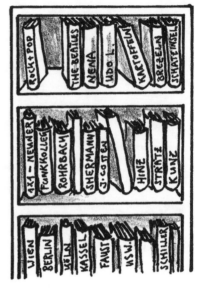

Intonation

9 Wortakzent: Markiere die betonte Silbe.

aufpassen · korrigieren · verstehen · anziehen · nachschlagen · Bildergeschichte ·
Kassette · Schokolade · Schokoladenfondue · Gesamtschule · japanisch ·
chinesisch · französisch · Kokosnuß · Schlagsahne · Erdbeeren · Kartoffelauflauf ·
Verabredung · international

10 Wortakzent: lang oder kurz?

	lang	kurz		lang	kurz
Rezept			Liste		
falsch			Tisch		
Sahne			Soße		
Zucker			Obst		
Schule			Kuchen		

11 Satzakzent: Markiere die betonten Wörter.

a ○ Entschuldigen Sie bitte, wie komme ich zur Jugendherberge?

● An der Kreuzung gehst du links, dann sind es nur noch hundert Meter.

b ○ Warum kommst du so spät? Was ist denn passiert?

● Ich habe meinen Geldbeutel verloren.

c ○ Kommst du heute abend mit ins Kino?

● Nein, ich muß noch Hausaufgaben machen.

Rechtschreibung

12 Fill in the missing letters.

a Ohne Text

WoXXenende · KlaXXe · EisenaXX · besuXXt · intereXXant · heiXX · FlasXXe · MineralwaX-Xer · groXX · BreXXeln · gegeXXen · FuXX · muXXt

_____

_____

_____

b Mit Text: Schreibe den Text ins Heft.

Lieber Jacques,

wir waren am WoXXenende mit der KlaXXe in EisenaXX. Wir haben dort die Wartburg besuXXt. Das war sehr intereXXant. Aber es war auch sehr heiXX. Ich hatte eine FlasXXe MineralwaXXer mit, die habe ich gleich getrunken. Dann hatte ich groXXen Hunger. Ich habe mir zwei BreXXeln gekauft und sie gegeXXen. Wir sind dann von der Wartburg zu FuXX zur Stadt gelaufen, eine Stunde lang.
Du muXXt bald kommen. Dann fahren wir zur Wartburg!

Dein Harald

Grammatik

13 Schreibe das Partizip II. Kontrolliere mit der Verbliste auf Seite 123.

sprechen	_____	verlieren	_____
singen	_____	notieren	_____
träumen	_____	anschauen	_____
zuhören	_____	schlafen	_____
üben	_____	lesen	_____

14 Was hast du gestern den ganzen Tag gemacht?

> schlafen · fernsehen · schlafen · telefonieren · einen Brief schreiben · lesen · Musik hören · essen · trinken

Gestern habe ich den ganzen Tag nichts gemacht. Ich war im Bett. Erst habe ich

_____. Dann habe ich _____. Dann habe ich wieder

_____. Dann habe ich mit meiner Freundin _____. Dann habe ich

meinem Freund _____. Dann habe ich mir ein Buch geholt und

2 Stunden _____. Dann habe ich noch _____. Dann hatte ich Hunger

und Durst: Ich habe mir Cola und Pommes frites geholt, bin wieder ins Bett gegangen und

habe ganz lange _____ und _____. Dann war ich wieder sehr müde

und habe wieder 5 Stunden geschlafen.

15 Perfekt mit *sein* oder *haben*?

laufen: _____ du schon einmal 100 Meter in 15 Sekunden gelaufen?

gehen: Ich _____ heute zu Fuß zur Schule gegangen.

spielen: Monika _____ gestern zwei Stunden Gitarre gespielt.

fliegen: Der Papagei _____ auf das Haus geflogen.

schwimmen: _____ du schon einmal einen Kilometer geschwommen?

geben: Wann _____ du mir das Buch gegeben?

aufgehen: Heute _____ die Sonne schon um 6 Uhr aufgegangen.

schlafen: Wie viele Stunden _____ du in der letzten Nacht geschlafen?

16 Modalverben: können, müssen, dürfen.

● Sandra, _____ du mir bitte helfen? Ich _____ die Hausaufgaben in Deutsch
  nicht machen!

○ Was _____ du denn machen?

● Wir _____ die richtigen Formen der Modalverben einsetzen.

○ Das ist doch einfach! Wie geht die Tabelle von „müssen"?

● Ich _____, du _____, er/sie/es _____, wir _____, ihr
  _____, sie _____.

○ Und von „dürfen"?

● Ich _____, du _____, er/sie/es _____, wir _____, ihr
  _____, sie _____.

○ Na also, du _____ doch alles! So, jetzt _____ wir ins Kino gehen.

Schreiben

17 Die Klassenparty

Eine Woche vor der Party. Die Klasse diskutiert mit Herrn Siebert, dem Klassenlehrer:
Was ist zu tun?

Daniel notiert:

> 1) Den Direktor besuchen, über die Party sprechen.
> 2) Hausmeister fragen, Räume anschauen.
> 3) Gute Musik suchen. Kassettenrekorder mitbringen.
> 4) Ideen für Spiele sammeln.
> 5) Klassenraum aufräumen.
> 6) Salate machen, Kartoffelsuppe kochen, ...
> 7) Freunde einladen

Eine Stunde vor der Party. Herr Siebert spricht noch einmal mit der Klasse. Haben wir alles gemacht?

1. Wir haben den Direktor besucht und über _____

2. _____

3. _____

4. _____

5. _____

6. _____

7. _____

18 Die Schatzinsel
Lies den Text, und zeichne den Weg zum Schatz in die Karte ein.

Das Vermächtnis des alten Piraten

„... du kommst von Westen. Fahre nicht zu nahe an die Insel in die Haifisch-Bucht. Dort gibt es gefährliche Korallenriffe. Segle um die Südspitze und wirf den Anker in der ‚Totenkopf-Bucht‘. Fahre mit dem Ruderboot an die südöstliche Land-zunge und gehe an Land ... Zwischen den Felsen gehst du ungefähr 100 Meter in Richtung zu einem großen Baum. Du findest ihn leicht – an ihm hängt ein Seil.

Rechts vom Baum ist die Hütte. Dort kannst du über-nachten.

Hinter der Hütte ist eine Brücke. Sie führt über eine Schlucht. Vorsicht, der Weg ist sehr schmal! Er führt dich in eine Höhle. Habe keine Angst! Gehe nicht nach links, dort haust ein wilder Löwe, und der Sarg von ‚Black Jack‘ liegt ne-ben einer Palme ... ‚Black Jack‘ wollte nicht auf mich hören, und dann kam der Löwe ..., aber was rede ich ...

Also, du gehst durch die Höhle bis zum Ausgang. Du siehst einen Turm. Klettere auf den Turm! Er steht mitten auf der Insel, und du hast die Hälfte des Weges schon zurückge-legt.

Schau nach Nord-Osten, du siehst den ‚Haifischkopf-Felsen‘. Das ist deine Richtung!

Wenn du vor dem Felsen stehst, schleiche dich vorsichtig um den Felsen. In der Nähe ist die Schlangenhöhle – sehr ge-fährlich!! Die Schlangen dürfen dich nicht hören!!

Hinter dem Felsen findest du einen Weg. Folge ihm! Er führt dich zwischen zwei Palmen hindurch zu einem Grab. Es liegt genau im Norden der Insel, John Silver hat dort seine Ruhe gefunden ...

Gehe an der Küste entlang nach Westen, bis zum Skelett – Vorsicht! Nachts spuken dort Geister!!

Stell dich neben das Skelett und drehe dich nach Süd-Osten. Folge der Richtung vom rechten Bein, zu zwei Palmen. Hinter den Palmen, zwischen Felsen, liegt der Schatz ...

Ich wünsche dir viel Glück ..."

Learning How to Read – A How-to Manual in Ten Steps

Let's begin with a German language text:

WISSEN: Sportliche Ereignisse

Foto: dpa/Witschel

Leichtathletik-WM in Rom 1987: Der Kanadier Ben Johnson siegt beim 100-Meter-Lauf der Männer.

Der Schnellste ...

Ben Johnson aus Kanada und Carl Lewis aus den USA sind bei den Leichtathletik-Weltmeisterschaften 1987 in Rom die schnellsten Läufer über 100 m. Lewis, vierfacher Olympiasieger, schafft die Strecke mit 9,93 sec. Johnson aber ist schneller: 9,83 sec. Ben Johnson wird mit brausendem Applaus gefeiert. Noch schneller wird er ein Jahr später bei den Olympischen Spielen sein, nämlich 9,79 sec. Bis sich wenig später herausstellt, daß der Kanadier gedopt war.

How much can you understand?

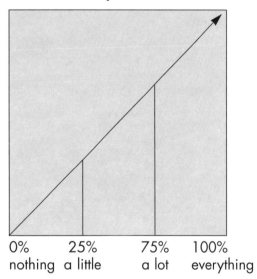

| 0% | 25% | 75% | 100% |
| nothing | a little | a lot | everything |

It is not easy to read some texts in a foreign language. There are many different problems, one of the biggest, new words! But you don't have to worry. Consider that you can already read well in English and that reading German is very similar. In *sowieso* we will help you to learn how to read German by providing you with help and practice, as well as Reading Tips.

When you read in English there are three important questions that you should always consider:

1	**Warum**	lese ich?	**Why**	do I read?
2	**Was**	lese ich?	**What**	do I read?
3	**Wie**	lese ich?	**How**	do I read?

Reading

1 Why Do I Read?

Write an example for each of the following possibilities.

a I read _____ because I enjoy it.

b I read _____ because I want to learn something.

c I read _____ because I have to (for school).

2 What Do I Read?

Every day more books are written, more newspapers are published, more texts appear.

Reading Test

Put a check in the correct column to indicate what you read every day, or in your free time, or even for school.

	never	sometimes	often
Comics			
Newspapers			
Novels			
Poetry			
Short stories			
Teen magazines			
School books			

Basic Rule > Good readers read a lot.

3 How Do I Read?

Most students read material in a foreign language differently than they read in English. One of the more important differences is reading speed.

Snail or Rabbit?

Look at both of the sentences below. Which method, shown by the pictures, do you think students use when reading a foreign language, which when reading English?

a Peter hat sich gestern drei neue Bücher gekauft.

b Yesterday Peter bought three new books.

Many students who read quickly in English read very slowly in German because they are afraid. They do not want to miss a word and they want to make sure they understand every word. But when you read word for word, your eyes must stop eight times in the German example sentence above and you do not see the words that come before and after the word you are reading. If you read three or four words together, the way you do in English, your eyes will only have to stop 2 or 3 times to read the sample sentence and you will always be looking at groups of words. You will always see the next word and this word may give you a clue to the meaning of the whole sentence.

Reading Tip ▷ A good reader does not focus on each individual word, but reads groups of words together.

There are certain Reading Strategies that can help you be a good reader. We will show you a few of them.

Reading

You automatically use reading strategies when you read in English. Here are three of the most important reading strategies.

Exercise: When do you use which strategy? Find an example for each of the strategies.

The Express Strategy
You quickly skim through a text to find out what it is about. You are not interested in details.

The Snoop Strategy
You read through a text, looking for specific information. The rest of the text is not important.

The Detective Strategy
You read the whole text very carefully, because all of the information is important to you.

Reading Tip Good readers use all three strategies when reading.

5 Why? – What? – How?   How to Use these Questions to Help You Read.

Why are you reading?

Situation 1
You like western movies the best and want to know if there are any on TV tonight after 6:00 PM.

Situation 2
You have to write a composition for school about the types of programs available on TV in your area. You want to know: Which programs are on every day? What type of programs are these?

Situation 3
You want to find the TV section of the newspaper.

KABELKANAL	RTL 2
7.54 Bim Bam Bino/Zeichentrick-Serien / 11.55 Tarzan / 12.55 Fantasy Island / 13.55 ● Zwei Freunde fürs Leben. (GB, 1968) / 15.45 Der Mann in den Bergen / 16.40 High Chaparral / 17.35 ● Wenn die Conny mit dem Peter. (s/w). (D, 1958) / 19.20 Bauerntheater: Thomas auf der Himmelleiter / 21.00 Die Straßen von San Francisco / 21.55 Hawaii 5-0 / 22.45 M.A.S.H. / 23.15 Murphy Brown / 23.45 ● Patty. (USA, 1987) / 1.25 Die Straßen von San Francisco / 2.20 M.A.S.H. / 2.45 Murphy Brown	8.25 Beverly Hills Teens / 8.55 C.L.Y.D.E. / 9.25 Peter Pan / 9.50 Ruck Zuck / 10.20 Bitte lächeln / 10.50 Benson / 11.25 Onkel Buck / 11.55 Hulk / 12.55 Hallo Kurt / 13.20 Mila Superstar / 13.50 Belle und Sebastian / 14.15 Die Erinnerungen des Esels Cadichon (1) / 14.40 Beverly Hills Teens / 15.05 C.L.Y.D.E. / 15.40 Peter Pan / 16.15 Abbott und Costello / 16.45 Fridolin / 17.00 Die 7-Millionen-Dollar-Frau / 17.50 Ruck Zuck / 18.20 Bitte lächeln / 19.00 Mensch Bachmann / 20.15 ● Wanda Nevada. (USA, 1979) / 22.25 ● Noch heute sollst du hängen! (USA, 1956) / 0.00 Twin Peaks

What are you reading?   The newspaper or TV magazine.

How do you read?   Express Strategy? Snoop Strategy?
                         Detective Strategy?

Exercise: Which strategy do you use for each of the above situations?

Situation 1 _____

Situation 2 _____

Situation 3 _____

Another example:

Why?   You and your friend want to go to the movies. You want to know what is playing and when.

What?   You pick up the newspaper and see all the different sections with articles about sports, culture, politics, etc.

How?   Which strategy or strategies do you need to use?

Express Strategy ☐

Snoop Strategy ☐

Detective Strategy ☐

> **Die Rache der Bikinier:** Ihre Heimat war ein Paradies. Dann kamen die Amerikaner und siedelten die Bewohner um.
> **Ein reiches Leben:** Grünwald, ein Vorort von München, ist die reichste Gemeinde Deutschlands.
>
> | | |
> |---|---:|
> | Fernsehen und Hörfunk | 25–26 |
> | Roman/Rätsel | 38 |
> | Sachbücher | 25 |
> | Ski-Journal | 48 |
> | Kino und Theater | 49 |
> | Familienanzeigen | 44 |
> | Mietangebote/-gesuche | 14–24/40 |
>
> Umfang dieser Ausgabe: 52 Seiten

Answer

First you use the Express Strategy to find the section and pages in the newspaper that you need: The Entertainment Pages. Then you use the Snoop Strategy to find the movie listings. You may not need to read the whole page because at the moment you are only interested in the movies. Finally you use the Detective Strategy to find a good movie playing at a time you and your friend can go.

Reading Tip ▷ Always begin to read using the Express Strategy. Only use the Detective Strategy when you absolutely must.

Reading

You can recognize many reading selections by their form. Remember the newspaper: The different sections – business, entertainment, sports, classified section – do not look alike. Look quickly at the following selections. Can you tell what kind of selections they are?

① Vorhin hat Peter „Blöde Kuh" zu mir gesagt!

② **Sportflugzeug abgestürzt Pilot bleibt unverletzt**

Bayreuth (dpa) – Mit dem Schrecken kam der Pilot einer Sportmaschine bei einer Bruchlandung beim oberfränkischen Mehlmeisel (Landkreis Bayreuth) davon. Die Maschine hatte beim Versuch einer Notlandung zunächst Baumwipfel ge-... teilte das

③ **Weitere Aussichten bis Dienstag**
Süddeutschland: Weiterhin wechselhaft und wieder milder. **Norddeutschland:** Am Sonntag bedeckt und Regen, am Montag wechselhaft mit Schauern, am Dienstag wechselnd bewölkt und weitgehend niederschlagsfrei. Tageswerte 4 bis 7 Grad.

2 Kinotage Montag u. Dienstag DM 8,-

Gloria-Palast
Karlsplatz 5, Telefon 555670

KASPAR HAUSER ab 12 Jhr., 2. Woche
13.00 / 16.30 / 20.00

Royal-Filmpalast
Goetheplatz 2, Telefon 533956/7

Mo./Di. (außer Feiertag) DM 9,-
MRS. DOUBTFIRE ab 6 Jhr. 1. Wo:
12.45/15.00/17.30/20.00/Do.-So. 22.30
THX-SOUND-SYSTEM + DOLBY STEREO
PERFECT WORLD ab 16 Jhr., 4. Wo.
14.00/17.00/20.00/Do.-So. 22.45
DIE DREI MUSKETIERE ab 12 Jhr. 1. Wo.

⑤ **MOSKAUER STAATSZIRKUS** Messeplatz

④ Denkt euch nur, die Erika verreist jetzt nach Amerika! Doch im Paß mit dem sie reist, ist ein Fehler, denn da heißt die Erika Sabina. Nun reist sie halt nach China.

⑥

Reading Tip ▷ If you know what kind of a text you have, you can often anticipate or guess what the content will be.

If you are going to read a weather report you expect to find certain words. Write down a few of the English words you usually find in a weather report.

_____

_____

_____

_____

Sturmböen, **Hessen, Rheinland-Pfalz, Saarland:** Überwiegend starke Bewölkung mit Schauern, zum Teil bis in die Niederungen als Schnee. Höchstwerte um 4, Tiefstwerte um 2 Grad. Böig starker Wind um West. **Nordrhein-Westfalen:** Wiederholt Regen- und Graupelschauer, örtlich auch kurze Gewitter. Tags um 5, nachts um 2 Grad. Stürmischer Wind um West. **Norddeutschland:** Stark bewölkt mit Schauern, zum Teil als Schnee oder Graupel, örtlich mit Gewittern. Höchstwerte 3 bis 5, Tiefstwerte um 2 Grad. Starker bis stürmischer Nordwestwind. **Ostdeutschland:** Wechselnd bis stark bewölkt mit Regen- und Graupelschauern, vereinzelt auch Gewitter. Tags 3 bis 5, nachts ... ad. M...

Look at the texts at the top of the page again. Match the sentences below with the correct texts above.

▶ Bei dem Unfall hat es keine Verletzten gegeben.
▶ Morgen wird es regnen.
▶ Der Film ist ab 16 Jahren.

▶ No people were injured in the accident.
▶ It will rain tomorrow.
▶ You must be 16 to see this film.

This exercise was not too difficult.

⚠ Remember that not every text form gives such good clues.

7 Learning to Recognize Signals in a Text

In every reading selection there are signals and clues that can help you to understand the text. You must learn to look for and recognize these signals.

The First Glance

The following are signals which help you to understand a reading passage. Try to find them before you start reading. You'll be amazed how much you can learn about the text. Let's try it. How much of the following text can you understand just from these clues?

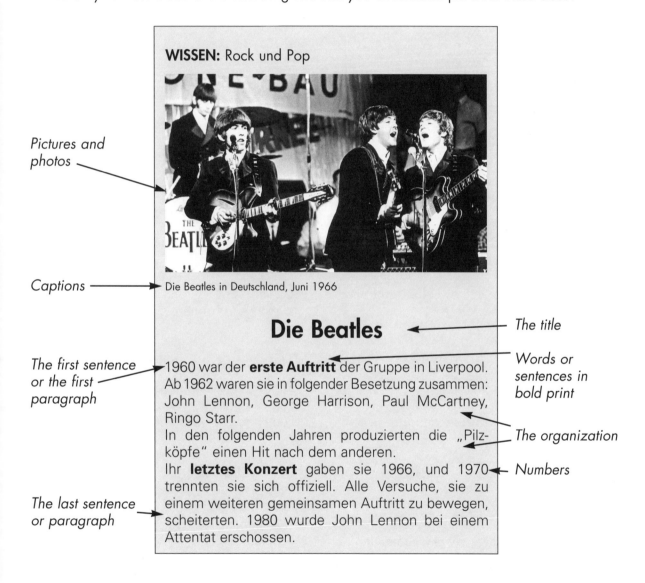

Pictures and photos

Captions

Die Beatles in Deutschland, Juni 1966

The title

The first sentence or the first paragraph

Words or sentences in bold print

The organization

Numbers

The last sentence or paragraph

WISSEN: Rock und Pop

Die Beatles

1960 war der **erste Auftritt** der Gruppe in Liverpool. Ab 1962 waren sie in folgender Besetzung zusammen: John Lennon, George Harrison, Paul McCartney, Ringo Starr.

In den folgenden Jahren produzierten die „Pilzköpfe" einen Hit nach dem anderen.

Ihr **letztes Konzert** gaben sie 1966, und 1970 trennten sie sich offiziell. Alle Versuche, sie zu einem weiteren gemeinsamen Auftritt zu bewegen, scheiterten. 1980 wurde John Lennon bei einem Attentat erschossen.

The Second Glance

Now it gets a little more difficult. There may be many new words. This can happen even when you are reading a text in English: think of a social studies book. A poor reader will reach for the dictionary and begin to use the Detective Strategy and read at a snail's pace. We'll show you how to be a better reader.

Reading

Reading Tip ▷ When you come across a new word, first try to guess its meaning through the context.

In English you automatically use the context in which new words appear to guess at their meanings. This is easy to try out. Take any text and cover up a sentence. Try to guess what the next sentence is after reading the previous sentence.

Example:

a

At the campground there are many boys and girls from different countries. They come from Italy, Germany ...

b

Dear Elke.
The weather here has been good but today ...

c

Hans is not a good student. His grades are very ...

Can you guess what comes next? Which words helped you?

This strategy also works well with German texts. The context and certain signals aid in your ability to figure out what the text means.

a Context: What comes before and after the unknown word?

Gestern XXX Peter im Kino. Er hat einen XXX gesehen.

b Words which you recognize.

– international words
– English words in German
– words from other languages

Mein Vater hat ein Restaurant.

English: *information*, German: *Information*
English: *garden*, German: *Garten*
French: *oncle*, German: *Onkel*

c Numbers are easy to recognize.

3000 Athletinnen und Athleten ...

d Grammar can also help. Words like "kein" or "nicht" change sentence meaning.

Heute kommt Susi nicht in die Schule.

e Nouns in German give a lot of information. They always begin with an upper case letter. You can often understand a text if you understand only the nouns.

... Sommer ... Familie Schmidt ... Italien ... Urlaub.
Im Sommer fährt Familie Schmidt nach Italien in Urlaub.

Reading Tip ▷ Only use the dictionary after trying other strategies.

9 Reading with a Plan: the ABC Plan

Now we would like to show you how to go about reading a German text.

 Pre-reading Phase

You begin to understand a reading selection before you actually begin to read. Remember the weather report? Before beginning to read you already knew a lot about the text.

Look at the reading selection below. When you look at the picture you already have clues as to what the text is about: technology, trains, locomotives. You can also guess that the text contains information about speed, the capabilities, the cost, or the benefits or problems with the pictured train. If you look closely at the picture you may even guess that the story contains something about the man who is looking out of the train window. By thinking about these things before you begin to read you will be able to understand the text faster.

Thinking about a text in this way helps you to understand. In addition, you should always ask yourself why you are reading and what you intend to do with the information you will get. A good example is the reading you do for some subjects in school. Very often there are questions about a reading selection in your textbook. Read these questions first, even though they may come after the selection. In this way you will be able to recognize the important information.

Reading Tip > Before you begin to read, think about the reading selection and look at any questions or assignments you must do. This is not cheating, this is a good study habit.

 Active Reading

Remember the exercise you did at the top of this page? Now read this selection quickly. Are your assumptions about this text correct? Now read the text a second time. This time read more slowly and pay attention to the signals and clues in the text.

Schneller Schienen-Express

Glück für den 13jährigen Peter aus dem hessischen Frankfurt. Der Eisenbahnfan durfte in der schnellsten Lokomotive Deutschlands mitfahren. Der neue Intercity-Express (ICE) hat 13 000 PS und fährt mit Tempo 250 quer durch die Bundesrepublik. Wie im Flugzeug gibt es auch im ICE viel Elektronik: Der Lokführer sieht auf einem Bildschirm, ob die Strecke frei ist. Der Zug fährt fast automatisch. Trotzdem gibt es keine Langeweile. Der Mann in der Lok kontrolliert alle Funktionen. Peters Kommentar: „Lokführer ist mein Traumberuf."

Reading Tip > Highlight the words and signals that help you to understand a text.

Post Reading Activities

What are you going to do with the information you have gathered by reading?

– You write notes for yourself because you don't want to forget the new information.
– You write notes because you want to give the information to someone else (for example a friend or your teacher).
– You write notes because you need to do some exercises or assignments based on the selection.

Here is a sample of some post reading exercises based on the text on page 103. Which reading strategy would you use to do these exercises? Put a check in the correct column.

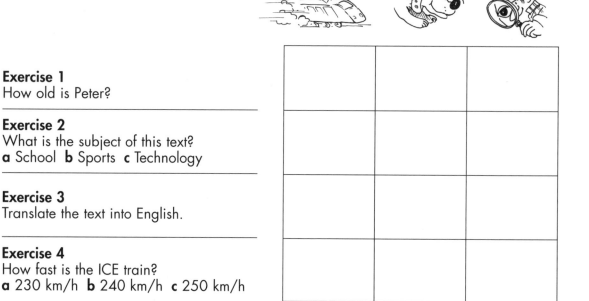

Exercise 1
How old is Peter?

Exercise 2
What is the subject of this text?
a School **b** Sports **c** Technology

Exercise 3
Translate the text into English.

Exercise 4
How fast is the ICE train?
a 230 km/h **b** 240 km/h **c** 250 km/h

What kind of reader are you?

Put a check in box **a** or box **b**.

1

a ☐ I always look at any pictures or headings first. Then I skim through the text so that I get an idea of what it is all about.

b ☐ I always carefully read through the whole text first. That way I know exactly what it is all about.

2

a ☐ I try to read a German text first without using a dictionary. There are many signals and clues in a text which help me to understand new words. Very often I can figure out the meaning of a sentence even when I don't know the meaning of two or three words at first. The context helps me to understand.

b ☐ I always use a dictionary when I am reading German. There are always so many words I don't understand that I must immediately look up in order to understand the text.

3

a ☐ I always first read my assignments or any exercises or questions I need to answer. Then I begin to read, knowing what I must pay attention to. In this way I know why I am reading a specific selection and if I need to read all of it or only a part of it. I also can choose which reading strategy I need to use.

b ☐ In school I always read the texts very carefully. Then I read and do the questions or the assignment. The questions are normally at the end anyway.

4

a ☐ I read a lot of different things: comics, novels, stories, magazines. I don't only read for school, I also read for fun.

b ☐ I only read for school because that way I can concentrate on learning. School books are more important than comics and magazines.

Evaluation

Only b:	Please read the Unit Learning *How to Read* again. Use the Detective Strategy.
1 x a:	You probably have problems with reading. Remember: Reading Strategies can help. Read the sections in this workbook again.
2 x a:	You are using some Reading Strategies but you can improve. Read the sections *Learning How to Learn* and *Learning How to Read* again.
3–4 x a:	You are a good reader. Continue in this way.

Learning to Listen:
A How-to Manual in 8 Steps

1 Let's Begin with a Little Experiment.

Listen to the cassette. What do you hear? Cars? Animals? Where is this scene taking place? Which characters can you identify?

Sounds produce pictures in our minds. What did you see while listening to the sounds on the cassette tape?

In reality you only heard a few sounds but your mind automatically puts the sounds into some sort of order. Out of this order you imagine pictures or even short films in your mind.

When listening, however, there is one big problem: The information comes quickly, like a camera flash, and then it's gone. Therefore it is very important to prepare ahead of time when you can.

Listening Tip Gather as much information about the listening text as you can, before you listen to it.

While you are listening there are other things you should do. We will give you some tips in our How-to Guide.

Listening Tip When listening, pay attention to voices, the tone of the voices and background noises. These things will help you to understand.

2 Problems

Think for a moment. What causes problems when you are trying to listen?
Which of the following is easier?

Read what the students below have to say about listening to German language texts.

I like to listen to German texts the best at home using my Walkman™. At home I have the time I need and it is quiet. I really have problems listening to German radio programs. Everything is too fast.
Nilgün, 13 years old

Whenever we listen to tapes in the classroom, I can ask questions. This helps me a lot. I don't like studying alone. In the classroom we can also listen more than once to the German text.
Florian, 11 years old

I often speak to German tourists. When I can see the person I'm talking to I can understand much better. I find speaking in German on the telephone to be a problem.
Beatrice, 12 years old

A friend once called me from Germany. That was a real problem. I could hardly understand anything she said. The only thing I really understood was that she wanted to come and visit me.
Vera, 13 years old

> **Listening Tip** ⟩ You have to prepare yourself to listen to German TV or radio.

3 Three Questions

Warum	höre ich?	**Why**	am I listening?
Was	höre ich?	**What**	am I listening to?
Wie	höre ich?	**How**	am I listening?

Try to quickly list the different types of texts you listen to in German and/or English.

in English	in German

Now you have a list of different kinds of listening texts. Whenever you hear these texts, you usually know within seconds what you are listening to: a sports announcement; the Top Ten; the news; a weather report; a dialog from your textbook. Why is this so? It is because listening texts, just like reading texts, have specific "forms". You must recognize the form to understand the message. The form gives you information about the content.

> **Listening Tip** ⟩ Try to find out before you hear a text, or at least in the first seconds while listening to a text, what type of text it is. Then it will be easier to understand the rest of the text.

Listening

Remember the ABC Plan for Reading? The Plan for Listening is similar.

A   Pre-listening Activities

What do I already know? (Names? Text?)
What am I going to hear? (Dialog? Music?)
What is the assignment? (Answer questions? Fill-ins?)
Read the assignment first.
If possible, talk about the listening text in class before listening to it.

It is best to do the above activities with your class. Now you know why you are listening, and what is really important.

B   Active Listening

Pay attention!
Do not try to write things down the first time you hear the text.
Pick out what is important for your assignment. Don't worry about other information.
Listen a second time, and take notes.

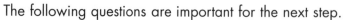

C   Post listening Activities

The following questions are important for the next step.

Why do you need the information?
What are you going to do with this information?
What can you remember?
What was especially important?

Exercise: Use the question list above and work with a listening text from your cassette. Answer all the questions before listening.

5 Listening Strategies

Listening strategies are also reading strategies. There are three of them:

Strategy	Activities	Results
Express Strategy 	You are looking for the sports news. You listen quickly to different stations. You are not interested in details, you are just trying to find the sports news.	You recognize the sports report immediately, because you have already listened often to sports news. You recognize quickly what the report is about and what information (scores for example) you will hear.
Snoop Strategy	You want to know the score of the last soccer match your team played. You listen carefully to the radio sports news until you hear the scores for this game. This is the information you wanted.	You heard some specific information, your team's game scores, because you concentrated on listening to this information. All the other sports news was not of interest to you.
Detective Strategy	You are a soccer fan. You listen carefully and try to remember all of the scores of all the games. Every detail is important to you.	You have understood a lot, but not quite everything. You didn't have to, but you still have more information with the Detective Strategy. Remember: Listening this carefully is not often done in everyday life.

Listening Tip ▷ A good listener uses strategies.

Always consider which listening strategy to use before you begin to hear the text. Ask your teacher for help.

6   Active Listening – An Example

Listening Exercises often look like the following (do not do the exercise until you have read the whole page):

Internationaler Campingplatz

Listen to the cassette and write down the country and city names.

	Land	Stadt
Rita Hinterberger		
Wolfgang Brauner		
Antonio Brandi		

Before you actually listen to the cassette use the ABC Plan:

What do you know about the situation before you begin to listen?
What might the people be talking about?

What information does this exercise give you that will help you choose your listening strategy? Which strategy will you use?

Express Strategy ☐

Snoop Strategy ☐

Detective Strategy ☐

Solution

For this exercise you need only concentrate on hearing the names of cities and countries. You use the Snoop Strategy.

Exercise: Find a listening exercise in the *sowieso* textbook. Consider which strategy you would use to do this exercise and discuss the strategy with your classmates.

7 Listening Quiz

You have earned a break and some entertainment.

Musik, Musik, Musik ...

Listen to the cassette. In what sequence do you hear the
different types of music? Write the numbers in the circles.

8 A Self-Test – What Kind of a Listener Are You?

Check off what is true or false for you.

Ja Nein

① I listen to the radio a little.

② I often listen to the radio, but only to music.

③ I often listen to news and sports on the radio.

④ Before turning on the radio, I think about what I want to listen to.

⑤ I often write down important things I hear on the radio.

⑥ Even if I don't understand what is on the radio, I don't immediately turn it off.

⑦ I listen to my German tapes at home.

⑧ I try to listen to German outside of the classroom whenever I get a chance.

⑨ I sometimes try to listen to German radio programs.

Evaluation

7 to 8 Ja-answers

OK! You're a very good listener. You won't have many problems listening to German. We wish you lots of fun.

4 to 6 Ja-answers

You're a good listener, but you can improve your skills. Practice listening to your cassettes or the radio. Concentrate!

Fewer than 4 Ja-answers

You are still not a very good listener. You should practice listening to the radio and cassettes and try asking yourself these questions: What do I want to listen to? What things are fun to listen to? How can I improve my listening skills? Which strategies should I use for the different things I listen to?

sowieso – Grammar

In *sowieso* the learning of grammar is done in three steps: Seek – Order – Structure.

Step 1 – Seek

The first thing you do in a unit is to work with a text. You might use a dialog or a newspaper selection to practice your speaking and writing skills. Sometimes in these texts there are new grammatical structures and often in order to use these new structures and communicate the new types of information, you will need to understand the grammar. To seek is to find the new grammar forms and structures, to underline them or write them down in a list. Your teacher will help you during this step.

○ Hi, Freddy, was machst du denn hier?
● Ich komme jetzt aus Wien. Und du, Sabrina?
○ Ich war gestern in Moskau.
● In Moskau? Ich bin im Juli in Moskau.
○ Im Juli bin ich in New York.
● Ja, in New York war ich auch. Da hatte ich Konzerte im Dezember und im Januar.
○ Im Januar war ich in Singapur. Warst du da schon mal? ...

Step 2 – Order

Now you take the structures you have noted and try to put them in some sort of order, thereby creating your own grammar tables. In this way you can best understand and learn the structures.

Ich	komme	jetzt	aus Wien.
Ich	war	gestern	in Moskau.
Ich	bin	im Juli	in Moskau.
Im Juli	bin	ich	in New York.

Step 3 – Structure

Now you can compare the structures you have discovered. Often you will be able to recognize and formulate the rules yourself. Sometimes we will give you tips to help you understand the grammar rules. Here is an example:

1	**2**		
Ich	komme	jetzt	aus Wien.
Ich	war	gestern	in Moskau.
Ich	bin	im Juli	in Moskau.
Im Juli	bin	ich	in New York.

You see that there are changes in the sentence structure when the reference to time comes before the subject and verb.

Learning Tip The rule you have discovered is: The verb is always in the second position regardless of what comes first.

The grammar tables in this section are already in order according to structures. You can always compare your own tables from your notebook with these tables. Sometimes there is a small table in the textbook. In this section you will be able to find more information.

In the grammar section you will find:

1   Nouns and pronouns

1.1 Nouns and the definite articles:	*der, das, die*
1.2 Nouns and the indefinite article:	*ein, eine*
1.3 Plural forms of nouns:	der Name – *die Namen*
1.4 Articles without nouns in a sentence (accusative):	○ Hast du einen Bleistift?
	● Ja, ich habe *einen.*
1.5 Compound nouns:	*das Deutschbuch*
1.6 Personal and possessive pronouns, masculine and feminine:	*ich* and *du* – *mein* and *dein*
1.7 Negation with nouns:	Das ist *kein* Fahrrad – das ist ein Moped.

2   Prepositions

2.1 Prepositions with the accusative:	*durch den Park, über die Brücke*
2.2 Prepositions with the dative:	*in der Bahnhofstraße, neben der Post*

3   Adjectives

3.1 Adjectives in sentences:	Amadeus ist *lieb.*
3.2 Comparison of adjectives:	*schön, schöner, am schönsten*

4   Verbs

4.1 Verb endings, present tense:	ich höre, du hör*st*
4.2 Separable prefix verbs:	*auf*schlagen
4.3 Negation:	Ich lerne heute *nicht.*
4.4 Command forms:	*Schlag* bitte das Buch *auf!*
4.5 Conjugation of the modal helping verbs:	ich darf, du mußt, sie kann
4.6 Modal helping verbs in sentences; questions and negation:	*Kannst du heute abend kommen?*
4.7 Helping verbs *sein* and *haben,* in the present and the *Präteritum:*	*war* und *hatte*
4.8 The *Perfekt* (formation):	*gegessen – gemacht – geschlafen*
4.9 The *Perfekt* used in sentences:	*Was hast du gestern gemacht?*

5   Sentence Structure: an Overview

5.1 Declarative sentence:	*Ich lerne Deutsch.*
5.2 Declarative sentence with time expression:	*Heute lerne ich nicht.*
5.3 Interrogative sentence with interrogative word:	*Wo ist der Ausgang?*
5.4 Interrogative without interrogative word:	*Lernst du auch Deutsch?*
5.5 Infinitive, participle, and verb prefix at end of sentence:	*Ich kann heute nicht kommen.*

Grammar

1 Nouns and Pronouns

1.1 Nouns and the definite article: *der, das, die*

Lerntip ▷ Nomen, Artikel und Bilder verbinden.

der

das

die

der
der Elefant, der Kuli

das
das Haus, das Buch

die
die Tänzerin, die Gitarre

Rules ▷ German nouns take one of three definite articles, *der, die, das*. This depends on the grammatical gender of the noun. *Der Kuli* is a masculine noun; *die Gitarre* a feminine noun, and *das Telefon* is neuter. Unlike in English where words do not have grammatical gender, in German we must learn the gender *(der, die, das)* of every noun when we learn the noun.

All words which end in *-ung* take the article *die:* die Zeichnung, die Begrüßung

Compound words: The last part of the word determines the article: der Lehrer + das Zimmer → das Lehrerzimmer

Plurals: All nouns in the plural take the article *die:* das Kaninchen – die Kaninchen, das Haustier – die Haustiere

Unit 3

1.2 Nouns and the indefinite article: *ein, eine*

	Singular		**Plural**	
der Computer	**ein** Computer		die Häuser	— Häuser
das Haus	**ein** Haus			
die Lehrerin	**eine** Lehrerin			

Rule ▷ *der* and *das* become *ein*, *die* becomes *eine*

1.3 Articles without nouns in a sentence (accusative)

Hast du einen Bleistift?
- Ja, ich habe einen.
- Nein, ich habe keinen.

Hast du ein Fahrrad?
- Ja, ich habe eins.
- Nein, ich habe keins.

Hast du eine Freundin?
- Ja, ich habe eine.
- Nein, ich habe keine.

Rules In German, we can make a positive statement in answer to a question in the same way we do in English.
Do you have a pen?   Yes, I have one.

We must pay attention to the *der, die, das* of the noun.

In German, when we answer negatively, we negate the noun and not the verb.
Do you have a pen?   No, I have none.

1.4 Plural forms of nouns: der Name – *die Namen*

A		B	
der Papagei	– die Papagei**en**	das Kaninchen	– die Kaninchen
die Frau	– die Frau**en**	der Computer	– die Computer
der Tourist	– die Tourist**en**	der Kilometer	– die Kilometer

C		D	
die Katze	– die Katze**n**	der Vogel	– die V**ö**gel
die Schule	– die Schule**n**	die Maus	– die M**äu**se
die Gitarre	– die Gitarre**n**	der Stuhl	– die St**üh**le

E		F	
der Hund	– die Hund**e**	das Auto	– die Auto**s**
das Pferd	– die Pferd**e**	die Disco	– die Disco**s**
das Telefon	– die Telefon**e**		

! die Freundin – die Freundi**nn**en

Most German nouns have plural forms similar to English words like *child – children, mouse – mice;* i.e. the plurals are different from the singular.

Learning Tip Always learn the plural form when you first learn the noun.

The plural forms are in the vocabulary list in the textbook.

Rules Nouns that end in *-o, -i, -a,* usually add an *-s* in the plural: die Disco – die Discos, das Taxi – die Taxis

Nouns which end in *-e* always add an *-n* in the plural: die Katze – die Katzen, die Schule – die Schulen

1.5 Compound nouns: *das Deutschbuch*

In German there are many compound nouns:

das Lehrbuch, das Arbeitsbuch, das Wörterbuch, der Bleistift, der Musikraum, die Turnschuhe, die Großmutter, der Taxifahrer, …

These words are made up of two or more parts:

The last word is always the root word: *das Buch.* (Ein Wörterbuch ist ein Buch.)
The first word is the modifier: *die Wörter.* (Other kinds of books: *das Deutschbuch* and *das Telefonbuch.*)

Rule ▷ A compound always takes the article of the root word: das Buch – das Wörterbuch.

Learning Tip ▷ Read compound words from the right to the left. The root word is always the last word on the right.

Can you think of some compound words in English?

In Units 3 and 17 in the textbook there are many compound words.

1.6 Personal and possessive pronouns, masculine and feminine: *ich* and *du* – *mein* and *dein*

○ Das ist mein Fahrrad!

● Nein, das ist mein Fahrrad!

Mine or yours – his or hers, these words tell us to whom something belongs.

Personal-pronomen	Possessivpronomen			
	maskulinum	**neutrum**	**femininum**	**Plural**
	der Hund	*das Fahrrad*	*die Schule*	*die Kaninchen*
ich	mein	mein	meine	meine
du	dein	dein	deine	deine
er	sein	sein	seine	seine
es	sein	sein	seine	seine
sie	ihr	ihr	ihre	ihre
wir	unser	unser	unsere	unsere
ihr	euer	euer	eure	eure
sie	ihr	ihr	ihre	ihre
Sie	Ihr	Ihr	Ihre	Ihre

Ich heiße Amadeus. Kiki ist **meine** Freundin. Wie heißt **dein** Freund?
Das sind **meine** Papageien, Koko und Lore.
Sind das **eure** Eltern? Nein, das sind nicht **unsere** Eltern, das sind **unsere** Großeltern.

Rule > Always add an -*e* for words that take the article *die*.
Die Katze – meine Katze

Unit 9

1.7 Negation with nouns: Das ist *kein* Fahrrad. Das ist ein Moped.

Nominative

der   ○ Ist das   ein Stuhl?
          ● Nein, das ist   **kein** Stuhl.

das   ein Fahrrad   –   **kein** Fahrrad

die   eine Schule   –   **keine** Schule

Plural: — Ferien   –   **keine** Ferien

Accusative

der   ○ Hast du   ein**en** Stuhl?
          ● Nein, ich habe **keinen** Stuhl.

das   ein Fahrrad   –   kein Fahrrad

die   eine Schule   –   keine Schule

Plural: — Ferien   –   keine Ferien

In a negation when you use *kein* it follows the same rules as the indefinite article
(see GR 1.2). *Kein* comes before the noun. In the accusative only the masculine article
(*der* – *kein*) changes form: *kein**en***.

Unit 5

Grammar

2 Prepositions

2.1 Prepositions with the accusative: *durch den Park, über die Brücke*

These two prepositions are used in *sowieso 1* with the accusative: *durch, über*

der Park
Gehe hier durch **den** Park und dann geradeaus.

die Brücke
Gehe zuerst über **die** Brücke und dann nach rechts.

Unit 19

2.2 Prepositions with the dative: *in der Bahnhofstraße, neben der Post*

These prepositions are used in the textbook with the dative: *zu, neben, hinter, vor, in, aus.*

	der Musikraum	**das** Lehrerzimmer	**die** Sporthalle	**die** Toiletten
Wie komme ich	**zum** Musikraum? (**zu** dem)	**zum** Lehrerzimmer? (**zu** dem)	**zur** Sporthalle? (**zu** der)	**zu den** Toiletten?

Wo sitzt Amadeus?

neben	hinter	vor	in

Wo ist die Klasse 7c?

Neben dem Musikraum.	**Neben** dem Lehrerzimmer.	**Neben** der Sporthalle.
Hinter dem Musikraum.	**Hinter** dem Lehrerzimmer.	**Hinter** der Sporthalle.
Vor dem Musikraum.	**Vor** dem Lehrerzimmer.	**Vor** der Sporthalle.
Im (in dem) Musikraum.	**Im** (in dem) Lehrerzimmer.	**In** der Sporthalle.

Rule ▷ When articles are used in the dative there is a change in all of them.
der → dem   die → der   das → dem

Plural
die → den (add *-n* to all nouns not ending in *-n*)

Unit 12

The preposition *aus*:

Singular	Das ist	die Schweiz. die Türkei. die Slowakei. die Bundesrepublik.	Ich komme	**aus der** **aus der** **aus der** **aus der**	Schweiz. Türkei. Slowakei. Bundesrepublik.
Plural	Das sind	die USA.	Ich komme	**aus den**	USA.
Länder ohne Artikel: Das ist Österreich			Ich komme	**aus**	Österreich.

Unit 2

3 Adjectives

3.1 Adjectives in sentences

Adjectives are words which modify nouns, or verbs (they are then called adverbs): *lieb, groß, alt.*

Amadeus ist *lieb*. Die Schule ist *groß*. Die Papageien sind *alt*.

3.2 Comparison of adjectives: *groß, größer, am größten*

You can compare things and persons using adjectives. The adjectives change when you do this. In English, for example we say *big, bigger, biggest* or *good, better, best.*

Juri ist 1,40 m *groß*. Jens ist *größer*. Er ist schon 1,75 m.

	Adjective	Comparative	Superlative
a	schwer klein lieb schnell lau**t**	schwerer kleiner lieber schneller lauter	am schwersten am kleinsten am liebsten am schnellsten am lau**te**sten
b	dumm schwach groß alt	d**ü**mmer schw**ä**cher gr**ö**ßer **ä**lter	am d**ü**mmsten am schw**ä**chsten am gr**ö**ßten am **ä**ltesten
c	gern viel gut	lieber mehr besser	am liebsten am meisten am besten

Rule If the adjective ends in *-t* you must add an *-e-* between the ending and the root word.

These adjectives have a vowel change.

These forms must be learned. They are like the English *good, better, best*. There are not many of them in German and in *sowieso 1* you will learn only three. (By the way: *gern* can only be used adverbially.)

Unit 17

Grammar

4 Verbs

4.1 Verb endings, present tense

Regular			Stem changing verbs: The vowels, and sometimes other letters change.	
ich	wohn**e**	kauf**e**	sprech**e**	les**e**
du	wohn**st**	kauf**st**	spri**chst**	lie**st**
er				
es	wohn**t**	kauf**t**	spri**cht**	lie**st**
sie				
wir	wohn**en**	kauf**en**	sprech**en**	les**en**
ihr	wohn**t**	kauf**t**	sprech**t**	les**t**
sie	wohn**en**	kauf**en**	sprech**en**	les**en**
Sie	wohn**en**	kauf**en**	sprech**en**	les**en**

Learning Tip ▷ Always learn the stem changing verbs with their changed form.
For example: *sprechen, er spricht* and *lesen, sie liest.*

When speaking, Germans often drop the final *e* in the first person singular (*ich*) form of the verb.

Ich wohn in Wien!

4.2 Separable prefix verbs

		Infinitive
Die Lehrerin ⟨liest⟩ einen Satz ⟨vor⟩		vorlesen
Aber die Schüler ⟨schreiben⟩ den Satz nicht ⟨auf⟩.		aufschreiben
⟨Kommst⟩ du am Sonntag ⟨mit⟩ ins Kino?		mitkommen
Ich weiß nicht. ⟨Rufst⟩ du mich heute abend ⟨an⟩?		anrufen
⟨Schlagt⟩ bitte eure Bücher ⟨auf⟩!		aufschlagen

This is similar to the English way of adding information to a verb. For example we say:

Call me **up** tonight.
Open your books **up**.

In German the additional part of the verb comes at the end of the sentence.

Learning Tip ▷ Always learn this type of verb in a sample sentence. For example: *aufschreiben – Sie schreibt den Satz auf.*

4.3 Negation: *Ich lerne heute nicht.*

Ich gehe nicht in die Schule, ich spiele nicht Fußball, ich mag keine Partys. Musik finde ich nicht gut und Deutsch will ich heute auch nicht lernen!

Rules

In a declarative sentence *nicht* is to the right of the verb.

Maria *geht nicht* gern in den Zoo.

In declarative sentences with helping verbs including modals *nicht* comes between the modal verb and the main verb.

Ich *habe* gestern *nicht gearbeitet.*
Fredo *kann nicht* Tennis *spielen.*

In English we usually place *not* between the helping verb and the main verb: *Maria is not going to the zoo. Fredo can not play tennis.* In German we do not use the helping verb *do* or *is,* therefore the negation in the present tense looks like "*Maria goes not to the zoo*".

4.4 Command forms, the Imperative: *Schlag bitte das Buch auf!*

Mach die Musik leiser, ich telefoniere!!

Learning Tip

German has three different forms for the imperative, just as it has three different forms of address; *du, ihr, Sie.* Learn how to use all forms.

Infinitiv	**Informell**		**Formell**
	Singular	**Plural**	
schreiben	Bitte **schreib** den Satz.	Bitte **schreibt** den Satz.	Bitte **schreiben Sie** den Satz.
hören	Bitte **hör** die Kassette.	Bitte **hört** die Kassette.	Bitte **hören Sie** die Kassette.
sprechen	**Sprich** bitte etwas lauter.	**Sprecht** bitte etwas lauter.	**Sprechen Sie** bitte etwas lauter.
vorlesen	Bitte **lies** den Text **vor**.	Bitte **lest** den Text **vor**.	Bitte **lesen Sie** den Text **vor**.
aufschlagen	**Schlag** bitte das Buch **auf**.	**Schlagt** bitte das Buch **auf**.	**Schlagen Sie** bitte das Buch **auf**.

Grammar

4.5 Conjugation of the modal helping verbs: *ich darf, du mußt*

	könnnen	müssen	dürfen
ich	kann	muß	darf
du	kannst	mußt	darfst
er			
es	kann	muß	darf
sie			
wir	können	müssen	dürfen
ihr	könnt	müßt	dürft
sie	können	müssen	dürfen

Rule Like some other verbs we have learned, the modals have a change in the verb stem when they are used in the singular forms.

Learning Tip The *ich* (first person singular) and *er, es, sie* forms of the modals are identical.

4.6 Modal helping verbs in sentences; questions and negation: *Kannst du heute abend kommen?*

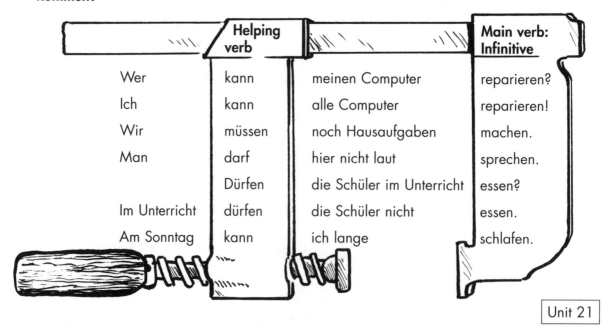

	Helping verb		Main verb: Infinitive
Wer	kann	meinen Computer	reparieren?
Ich	kann	alle Computer	reparieren!
Wir	müssen	noch Hausaufgaben	machen.
Man	darf	hier nicht laut	sprechen.
	Dürfen	die Schüler im Unterricht	essen?
Im Unterricht	dürfen	die Schüler nicht	essen.
Am Sonntag	kann	ich lange	schlafen.

Unit 21

Rule Helping verbs appear where the main verb normally does, always in the second position. Helping verbs then normally need a second element, the infinitive completer, at the end of the sentence. If the main verb is understood, German speakers sometimes omit it. For example: *Kannst du Deutsch (sprechen)?*

4.7 Helping verbs *sein* and *haben* in the present and the *Präteritum* (past tense): *ich war, ich hatte*

	sein		*haben*	
	Präsens	Präteritum	Präsens	Präteritum
ich	bin	war	habe	hatte
du	bist	warst	hast	hattest
er				
es	ist	war	hat	hatte
sie				
wir	sind	waren	haben	hatten
ihr	seid	wart	habt	hattet
sie	sind	waren	haben	hatten

Kommst du mit schwimmen?

Ich war schon!

Unit 14

4.8 The *Perfekt* (conversational past tense)
The past participle of the irregular verbs found in *sowieso 1*:

Infinitiv	Partizip II	Infinitiv	Partizip II	Infinitiv	Partizip II
abschreiben	abgeschrieben	gießen	gegossen	schneiden	geschnitten
anfangen	angefangen	haben	gehabt	schreiben	geschrieben
anrufen	angerufen	heißen	geheißen	schwimmen	geschwommen
ansehen	angesehen	helfen	geholfen	sehen	gesehen
anziehen	angezogen	herausnehmen	herausgenommen	sein	gewesen
aufgehen	aufgegangen	kennen	gekannt	singen	gesungen
aufschlagen	aufgeschlagen	kommen	gekommen	sitzen	gesessen
aufschreiben	aufgeschrieben	können	gekonnt	sollen	gesollt
aufstehen	aufgestanden	laufen	gelaufen	sprechen	gesprochen
aussehen	ausgesehen	leihen	geliehen	stehen	gestanden
aussprechen	ausgesprochen	lesen	gelesen	tragen	getragen
beginnen	begonnen	liegen	gelegen	treffen	getroffen
beschreiben	beschrieben	mitbringen	mitgebracht	trinken	getrunken
bleiben	geblieben	mitgehen	mitgegangen	tun	getan
durchlesen	durchgelesen	mitkommen	mitgekommen	verbinden	verbunden
dürfen	gedurft	mitschreiben	mitgeschrieben	vergessen	vergessen
einladen	eingeladen	mögen	gemocht	vergleichen	verglichen
essen	gegessen	müssen	gemußt	verlieren	verloren
fahren	gefahren	nachschlagen	nachgeschlagen	verstehen	verstanden
fernsehen	ferngesehen	nachsprechen	nachgesprochen	vorlesen	vorgelesen
finden	gefunden	nehmen	genommen	vorsprechen	vorgesprochen
fliegen	geflogen	raten	geraten	waschen	gewaschen
geben	gegeben	rauslassen	rausgelassen	weitergehen	weitergegangen
gefallen	gefallen	reiten	geritten	wissen	gewußt
gehen	gegangen	schlafen	geschlafen	zurückfliegen	zurückgeflogen
gewinnen	gewonnen	schlagen	geschlagen		

Unit 20

Learning Tip ➤ Always learn the past participle together with the infinitive of verbs.

Grammar

4.9 The *Perfekt* in sentences: *Was hast du gestern gemacht?*

	Bist	du gestern abend im Kino	gewesen?
Nein, ich	habe	keine Zeit	gehabt.
Ich	habe	gestern mein Fahrrad	repariert.

Unit 18

Learning Tip ▷ The past participle is easy to find: In a main clause it always appears at the end and the helping verb *haben* or *sein* appears in the second position normally occupied by the main verb. This is similar to the infinitive with modal helping verbs.

---

5 Sentence structure

5.1 The declarative sentence

1	2	
Ich	(lerne)	Deutsch.
Meine Schwester	geht	in Klasse 9a.

Rule ▷ The verb is always in the second position.

5.2 Declarative sentence with time expression: *Heute lerne ich nicht.*

1	2	
Ich	(war)	im Kino.
Gestern abend	war	ich im Kino.
Ich	fahre	in die Stadt.
Heute nachmittag	fahre	ich in die Stadt.
Ich	besuche	meine Tante.
Morgen	besuche	ich meine Tante.

Rule ▷ The verb remains in the second position even if the declarative sentence starts with a word other than the subject.

Unit 14

5.3 Interrogative sentence with interrogative word: *Wo ist der Ausgang?*

1	2	
Wer	(hat)	noch 10 Mark?
Wie	heißt	dein Freund?
Wo	wohnt	Maria Anderl?
Was	machst	du am Wochenende?
Wann	gehst	du schwimmen?

Unit 4

5.4 Interrogative sentence without interrogative: *Lernst du auch Deutsch?*

(Hast)   du Englisch gelernt?

(Willst)   du auch Französisch lernen?

(Wart)   ihr schon in Österreich?

(Kommt)   Peter auch mit ins Kino?

Rule ▷ When asking questions which can be answered with yes or no, the verb is in the first position.

Unit 4

5.5 Infinitive, participle, and verb prefix at end of sentence: *Ich kann heute nicht kommen.*

Maria	hat	Jens gestern	angerufen.
Mit 14	dürfen	Jugendliche nicht	rauchen.
Die Schule	fängt	um 8 Uhr	an.
	Hast	du die Hausaufgaben	gemacht?
Wo	kann	ich den Direktor	finden?
	Hört	euch die Kassette	an!

This is a summary of Grammar points 4.4, 4.6, and 4.9. Notice that the verb completer (infinitive, separable prefix, or past participle) always goes to the end of a sentence or main clause and that the helping verb, unless it is a question which can be answered with yes or no, always appears in the second position.

page

20 Reisepaß, Tourist: L. Rohrmann; Computer, Telefon:
Th. Gockel, C. Knobel, grafic fotografie, Hofgeismar

36 Th. Gockel, C. Knobel, grafic fotografie, Hofgeismar

42 L. Rohrmann

46 Interfoto, München

48 Kümmerly und Frey, Bern

58 Lindenberg SZ Archiv

59 Nena: Sony Music

61 L. Rohrmann

62 Krokodile: H. Funk; Affen, Kamel, Hund, Eisbären:
L. Rohrmann

64 L. Rohrmann

67 A: Interfoto, München; B: T. Scherling; C: B. Stenzel

71 Wencke, Daniel: H. Funk, Familie: Jugendscala 3/88,
Frankfurter Societätsdruckerei; Heike: L. Rohrmann

75 Karte Polyglott, München

76 Stadtplan Düsseldorf: aus: "Gästeführer Düsseldorf",
Ewald Schwarzer Verlag, Taufkirchen

77 Fabrik: Opel Eisenach, GmbH; Bachhaus: Bachhaus
Eisenach

79 Wartburg: aus: Stadtführer Eisenach 1990, Dr. Wolfram
Hitzeroth Verlag, Eisenach; Steinberghaus: Naturfreunde,
Münden

page

82 Fotos Scherling

85 Fußabdrücke Mond: Süddeutscher Verlag, Bilderdienst,
München

95 Der Schnellste ..., Leichathletik:
Velber Verlag, Seelze

96 Th. Gockel, C. Knobel, grafic fotografie, Hofgeismar

100 Lieschen (ein Bild): aus: Erich Rauschenbach, Aare
Verlag, Solothurn 1979, in: Edition Goethe, Junge
deutsche Literatur

101 Die Beatles: Velber Verlag, Seelze (Text); Süddeutscher
Verlag, Bilderdienst, München (Foto)

103 Schneller Schienen Express: GCI Ringpress (Foto), Juma
3/91 (Text)

106 H. Funk

107 H. Funk

111 Bach: Deutsche Grammophon, unter Verwendung
eines Gemäldes von Horemann (Archiv für Kunst und
Geschichte); Boarischer Tanzbodn: M. Well, München

119 H. Funk

Show this to your teacher!

Grammatik ganz neu: Grammatikbogen

Fiktionale Texte mit Aufgaben und Lösungsschlüsseln für den Unterricht Deutsch als Fremdsprache

Der Grammatikbogen enthält wie der vom gleichen Team erstellte **Lesebogen** eine Sammlung didaktisch aufbereiteter literarischer Texte in 3 Schwierigkeitsgraden: 27 Unterrichtsentwürfe mit Aufgaben zu allen wichtigen grammatischen Themen der Grundstufe können in der Klasse ohne weitere Vorbereitung des Lehrers eingesetzt werden. Die selbständige Bearbeitungsmöglichkeit macht den **Grammatikbogen** darüber hinaus auch für den Selbstlerner einsetzbar.

Von K. van Eunen, J. Moreau, F. de Nys,
B. Stenzel und M. Wildenbeest.
192 Seiten, DIN A4, im Ringordner
ISBN 3-468-49478-5